LIEUTENANT COLONEL "BOOM" MARSAW: BORN to RUN

*

AN AUTOBIOGRAPHY
of a
CANADIAN MILITARY LEADER

Thorold Marsaw

LIEUTENANT COLONEL "BOOM" MARSAW: BORN to RUN

Edition: This autobiography is a revised, edited version of the 1999 work by Thorold Marsaw, "Born to Run: My Story".

Dedication: This book is dedicated to the multitude of men and women who have given their lives to advance peace in the world, to all of my supporters, mentors, teachers and family -- most especially to my wife and companion Irene, who has lived so many adventures with me -- and to my all sustaining God and Saviour.

Accuracy: To present the information as accurately as possible, the actual names of people and places have been used, as well as memory allows. No other information will be provided about such persons without their express permission.

Appreciation is sincerely expressed to the editor and cover designer of this edition, James Pittaway, and to the reviewers.

Bibliographic entry:
>Marsaw, Thorold (2013). Lieutenant Colonel "Boom" Marsaw: Born to Run. Brantford, Ontario, Canada. JP Enterprises, 158 pp.

Published by JP Enterprises, 36 Hansford Drive, Brantford, ON. N3S 0B6 519-304-2272

Printed and Distributed in Canada by Essence Publishing 20 Hanna Ct., Belleville, ON. K8P 5J2. 1-800-238-6376

TABLE of CONTENTS

PREFACE

At this point in my life, there are few things that I would rather do than sit down with my parents and have them share the experiences of their days. At the time when that was possible, I was far too busy, too absorbed in living out the adventure that was my own life, to consider what they might have had to share.

What I have undertaken here is to provide my children and any others who might be interested, with a thumbnail sketch of my world. There is so much more I could say. Indeed every line tends to give birth to further remembrances.

Whether the challenges and excitement were more or less rich and rewarding than I have portrayed them to be, you cannot prove it by me. Certainly I have learned in life that the fullness of any given moment can seldom be realized until an opportunity has been taken to reflect upon it.

And when you do reflect on it, you realize once again that the foundation is critical to any life or structure, so I will share some of the early experiences that shaped the life that was to be, as well as many of the events of my military career.

If, in the passage of time, my memories and reflections have matured a little, I hope that you will not find that to be intolerable. The intent of my words is to give expression to my thanksgiving unto God for the life with which He has blessed me.

- Thorold Marsaw

Chapter 1

A REAL "BOOM"?

The gruff voice on the phone growled, "Marsaw?"

"Yes sir, General!"

"Marsaw -- I got a report that somebody had blown up a bridge! Now, usually I'd put this down to just a bad rumour, but when your name was attached to it I knew I'd better check it out."

"Yes, sir."

"What do you know about it?"

"Well, sir, we did blow up a wooden trestle bridge yesterday."

"A trestle bridge? Not just any little old bridge but you had to blow up a high, wooden trestle bridge? Good God, just because you're nicknamed Boom doesn't mean you have to go around blowing things up!"

"Well, I..."

"Don't interrupt! And another thing. Did you happen to notice that this is Canada, not Korea? You blew up a Canadian trestle bridge? I'm not sure I really want to know but what's this all about?"

"Well, General, this was a training exercise -- and yes, I had permission to remove an old, abandoned bridge, only about six stories high, right next to the new one -- because our men need real experiences so they know what to do when they're in a real war, and you know that good training can save lives, and they're about the best trained, and..."

　　　　...but I'm getting a long way ahead of myself.

Let me go back to the beginning -- to many of the experiences
that led to:
>   my nickname,
>>   that trestle bridge,
>>>   and far beyond...

Chapter 2

IN THE BEGINNING

"Don't slam the screen door!"

As usual the appeal came too late, for I was already in flight, the door on its way to closing and my hand well past the point of intervention. "Sorry, mom." was the best I could do to right the wrong. The consolation was that the bang usually heralded a significant period of respite for my dear mother. It was unlikely that she would hear from me again until my body's fuel tank ran low and I returned for my not infrequent top-ups.

"That boy was born with running shoes on!" she would remark to her friends. "A perpetual motion machine if ever there was one."

But I'm getting ahead of myself again. Even early experiences are critical to the making of a good soldier, so here goes!

I can say, as a friend of mine once remarked, "I was born at a very early age." To be specific, I was born at Victoria Hospital, London, Ontario, August 10, 1931, just in time for lunch as my mom always delighted in reminding me. For the longest time I thought that I held pretty exclusive claim to that date. It would be many years before I met someone who had the same birthday. The painful truth is that I share it with some 16,438,300 other souls, all of whom are every bit as significant as I.

With that sobering realization in hand and not wishing to lose all claim to fame, I took to listing major historical events with which I shared that date in history. For instance, it was the occasion of the first reading of the American Declaration of Independence in Savannah, Georgia, in 1776. It was the moment when the first long distant phone call was made from Brantford to Paris, 1876, and the day on which WW1 broke out in 1914.

Actually, August 10th isn't the most important date in my life. The most important was the one on which I was born again. I was only knee high to a grasshopper when I first came to the realization of who the Lord Jesus is and what He had done for me. The exact day has faded from memory but I'm sure it was during family devotions. Mom often gathered my sister Margaret and me to her for a few moments around the Word and in prayer before she launched us off to school. I was about six or seven at the time.

My childhood and the years of my youth were filled with unending adventures. Faithfully mom would strive to remind me of the presence of God and the evidence of His goodness. She would seize opportunities to use the little things of life to teach the great truths of the Lord. And she lovingly administered her own brand of discipline. Wouldn't our world be a whole lot better today if more kids were sent off to wash their mouths out with soap?

Most significant to this unfolding tale is the knowledge that I grew up during the horrendous years of WW2. My father twice tried to enlist and was twice rejected. It just about tore him apart, although I'm sure that my mother must have breathed a great sigh of relief.

Needless to say, I really had no idea of the horrors of war and therefore nothing to temper my youthful enthusiasm about the whole business. I wanted to go. I wanted Hitler to know that when he decided to mess around with the Empire, he'd bitten off more than he could chew! It was going to cost him big! And I wanted to be in on the collection!

I ate and slept war. Each week the *Star Weekly* contained up-to-date maps and sketches showing how things were going. While most of the guys my age had pin-ups on their bedroom walls, mine were covered with battle maps. When mom gave us chocolate pudding or Jell-O for dessert I used to drive her crazy in the way I would attack my dish. I would plunge in my spoon and scoop out a hefty portion, remarking as I did, "The British have landed here." Back into the pudding for "The Americans landed here." And of course, reserving an appropriately large portion, I would scoop out a spot to define where the Canadians had gone ashore. Every day was D-Day!

"Will you cut that out?" mom would appeal.

Dad quietly endorsed my spirit. He wrote poems to encourage the nation and urge us not to wane in the pursuit of our mission. I don't have copies any longer, but as the Russians launched their spring campaign, the first part of that year's work went something like this.

> The Bear is up from her winter sleep,
> It's time this country took a peek,
> To see what's going on around,
> Before the Axis gets us down.

Childhood adventures? Ah yes, there was the time I got "the strap". Why this should be the first thing to come to mind I have no idea, but now is as good a place as any to deal with the matter. It was administered to me by a teacher named Jack Metler, a family friend and a fine Christian.

You see, I'd been caught in the washroom with a couple of guys who had gone there for a drag or two. No, I wasn't smoking. I just happened to be in the wrong place at the wrong time. Before he gave me my whacks, Jack explained what a favour he was doing me. If I didn't get it and the word got out, and it would get out, then I would be on the receiving end of the ridicule of my peers. He assured me that that would be a fate far worse than three licks of the best he'd hand out.

Okay, okay Jack, but did you have to hit me as hard as the bad guys? Couldn't you have faked it just a little?

Are you asking if I had a go at smoking? The short answer is yes, but thank God I got sick on my first try and never went back for seconds. The whole idea wasn't really very inviting. Have you ever had a look at a pipe cleaner after it has done its thing? My dad was never able to beat the habit, so I had a first hand awareness of that little operation.

In grade six I had Miss Pulfas. My Christmas report card dubbed me the worst kid ever to occupy a chair in her classroom! I don't know how my parents responded to that one. Maybe the consequence was so traumatic that my mind has chosen to just blot out the whole dreadful experience. Somehow I would think that they might have chosen to apply a little of the board of education to the seat of learning, but I really can't remember. Oh! There is another chapter to this tale. By year end Miss Pulfas wrote, "I have never been more wrong about a boy in all my life." Thank you, Lord. Thank you for whatever lessons that year most certainly held.

Just in case you might not have caught the right message, I loved school. Mind you, I'm not saying there wasn't the odd occasion when I didn't feel like going. When mom consented to my staying home, she would also insist that I spend the time in bed, that being the best place to recover from whatever it was that ailed me. Unless I was really sick, I could only take a few moments of that before I would be up and going, if needs be running all the way to school just so I wouldn't be late. I didn't really want to miss any of the fun and every day had its share of fun. Good teachers have a knack of making learning that way; good friends put the icing on the cake.

I need to say that down through the years many of my best friends have been teachers and many a lady teacher has been the object of my affection. Haven't you noticed how pretty they are? As with many young boys, I was always falling in love.

But let's leave the classroom for a time. Let me tell of the day I broke off my two front teeth playing hockey. I'm sure glad I was smiling at the time. The puck didn't touch anything else as it passed by. When I got home that evening, the back door was locked. That was most unusual. Dad came to let me in, and wondering at the peculiar way I was standing he asked, "What happened to you? Did you lose your front teeth?"

Now, how did he know that? I've raised five kids and I've never been able to muster the insight that my mom and dad seem to have had in respect to the whys and wherefores of kids. It beats me. They were uncanny!

Next day, I spent four hours in a dental office. Doctor Baker was the guy who undertook to straighten out the mess. He yanked out the nerves, put in temporary plugs and booked me to return the following week.

As I remember, it was about three and a half years before I got up enough courage to go back for round two. But now, would you believe that in recent times I have actually fallen asleep in a dental chair? Just call me "Cool-hand Luke".

Getting back to my parents' child raising skills, I must point out that they really worked at the job. Dad had been a goalie in his youth and I loved it when he came down to the local rink and let us guys shoot at him. He was good.

Then too, he pitched for his company team in the industrial softball league. After supper, I would stand in front of the garage door and try to catch for him. He was really good.

One summer, on dad's holiday week, we jumped on our bikes and rode all the way to Brantford. Not many dads would do that. He managed to keep up fairly well too. He was really pretty good for an old guy. I didn't think about it at the time, but I bet he was glad to get back to work. Things were just a wee bit less tasking there. By the way, that was the only occasion on which I remember meeting my Gramma Marsaw whom we had gone to visit. With no car or phone, maintaining any meaningful contact was nigh impossible.

Both of my grandfathers were gone before I was born, but my grandmother on mom's side lived in London, so I saw her a fair bit. She and my step-grandfather owned a large old home not far from London's Victoria Park. They took in boarders to help meet expenses, but there was still much of the house to which I had access. The best part was the attic.

Have you ever been in an attic? You know, someone ought to pass a law making it mandatory for every house to have one. I mean, one you can play in. It is one of life's most wonderful inventions! Attics are like tree houses. They are the stuff from which great adventure is spawned with dusty trunks, photo albums, tiny windows through which you can spy upon the world and, oh yes, spider webs.

Something else my grandparents had which was very special was a car with a rumble seat. What's that, you say? Well, it's a bit like having a seat fitted in the back of a small pick-up -- a sort of convertible with no top. When it rained you threw a piece of tarp over your head, leaned as close to the back window of the cab as you could and had the time of your life. You always got soaking wet and after a while you usually just stopped trying to keep dry and enjoyed the experience.

Over the years I put a pile of miles on my bikes. The trip to Brantford wasn't the only long distance venture. I remember going to Goderich with a couple of buddies. That was a little over 100 km. We slept under the stars on the high ground, overlooking the dock where they loaded grain into the huge freighters.

There was a longshoreman's strike and all night the fellows were picketing. We pretended we were spies. Our task was to keep an eye on the strikers to be sure they didn't do any vandalism. I'm sorry to have to report that we didn't do a very good job, for at one point I woke up and found the other guys were all asleep. It was a good thing we weren't in the Army. I think a guy can be shot for sleeping on sentry duty!

What life story would be complete without a least one remembrance of Christmas? I need to start by telling you that I love secrets. But there is one thing I love better: telling them! I can't remember the year, probably around 1938, but I know I was very young. Mom and I went shopping for dad's gift: a guitar. His family was very musical and he once had his own guitar but it had been long gone.

Well, she carried the instrument home, hid it behind the chesterfield and swore me to secrecy. I'm not sure how long I was able to keep that wonderful surprise bottled up. It was at least a day. And I'm not sure how I came to spilling the beans, nor why, but it came out. Mom was some upset! She took after me, chasing me all over the place. She couldn't run fast and certainly couldn't catch me, but to put an end to it, I took up refuge behind dad who, at this point, was having the time of his life. Mom might have been crying a little; she did that every once in a while. Those tears had a unique way of gripping my heart. I couldn't stand it when my mom cried. Those tears told me that I had crossed the line, mom was really hurting and I'd best get things right. Oh, the power of a woman's tears -- of a good woman's tears!

You know that it's an ill wind that doesn't blow some good. Dad was far enough along in renewing his talent that he did a pretty good job playing his new guitar for us, as we sang carols on Christmas day.

Gift giving was another one of those things that gave birth to a wonderful truth. At Christmas or the likes, I'd ask mom what gift she would like. Her answer was always the same: "Just be a good boy."

"Ah, mom, I can't buy that." The implication of my response was that I would be good, but I wanted to give her something more tangible. The truth of the matter is that there's nothing more tangible, nothing of greater substance. It was years later, indeed in the midst of raising my own family, that I came

13

to the realization of just what a wonderful gift the good behavior of your children really is. Mine weren't bad! They must have gotten that from their mom. They certainly didn't learn it from me! Thank you, Irene.

Please be aware that these events are not in chronological order. I'm recording them pretty much as they come to mind.

It was in my very early years that I almost did my dear dad in. Often I would go to meet dad at the bus stop where he got off on his way home from work. That way I could carry his lunch bucket home and, by right of possession, had first dibs on any leftovers.

One day I was a bit late and he was already making his way along the path that led home. When I reached him he was on his hands and knees. I thought that he wanted to play horsey so I jumped on. What had actually happened was that he had hurt himself at work.

As he was walking along, he had suffered a terrible cramp in his back and had gone down to try to ease the pain. At the time it was a near death experience. Years later it was looked upon as a precious moment in our relationship. We did have some great times!

Oh yes, somewhere in the midst of all this, I remember being at the service during which my mom and dad were baptized. I would think that I might even have been a pre-schooler at the time, yet the event still lingers in my recollection. Such is the power of the testimony of baptism by immersion.

On we go. Let me tell you of the time I fell off the second story roof of our home. My sister and I had been sent to our rooms because we had been misbehaving. We had the brilliant idea that I could slip out my window, work my way along the roof and into her room, where we could pick up right where we had left off before being so rudely interrupted.

Slip along the roof was right! I didn't make it. But I did experience the grace of God for, while I fell right onto a rock garden, I walked away unscathed. In fact my life was to hold a series of such experiences. I've been in three forced airplane landings and a couple of pretty scary vehicle accidents. My worst injury in the military was little more than a scratched elbow and gnarled leg. But we'll come back to some of that later.

I can't remember too much of what my sister and I did (she was older than I was). If she were still around, you could ask her. One thing that comes to mind, however, is the great time we had when bottles of this or that came to an end. We would make up exotic concoctions. For instance, on one occasion a bottle of corn syrup was declared to be all gone. We turned it upside down on a saucer and left it for a while.

When we went back to check we were rewarded with a little puddle of syrup. What all we mixed in I don't recall. Certainly Ketchup was one of the ingredients. It added a nice red tone. Maybe some Rice Krispies. The end product was about as much fun to eat as it was to lick out mom's mixing bowls. That was always a happy occasion!

I need to mention that I was born in the midst of the Great Depression. Most people were hurting and my family was no exception. When I was about six, we lost our home. In the next thirteen years as we scrambled to regain our footing, we lived in nine different abodes. There were a one-room on the third floor of an old rooming house, a tiny apartment over a service station, houses that were in the flood plain of the Thames, one that was roach infested, and on and on.

When dad had defaulted on the mortgage, they repossessed the house and put it on the market. When it sold, he owed the difference between that price and what he had originally agreed to pay for it. Back in the depression, such homes went for fire-sale prices, so the difference was quite substantial. Bankruptcy was out of the question. Dad believed that going that route ruined the person for life. It was nearly a decade before he managed to pay off the outstanding debt.

When we finally got back into owning a home, it was a modest bungalow on Princess Avenue -- a house with no basement. Dad and I proceeded to create one by hand. Boy was that back-breaking work, but a wonderful indicator that we were once again on the way up!

Just maybe we were poor, but I never knew it. We always had enough to give a sandwich and a drink to anyone who came by asking for a handout. Mom could never say no. And true to His word, God always made sure there was enough to let it happen. Dad worked as a mechanic for the London Street Railway. I remember him talking about the fellows at the shop going after a pay increase. It sounds almost ludicrous today, but they were asking for five cents an hour more and had to settle for three. Mind you now, if I recall correctly children's bus tickets were only two for a nickel.

Every once in a while, dad had the responsibility of getting the bus and streetcar fleet out on the road for a Sunday. Sometimes I was allowed to go with him. Boy I loved that! I got to raise the big doors on the parking garages and clang the warning bells on the streetcars. Lots of drivers got to know me and often they let me ride free. That gave me a real sense of belonging. You see, employees had passes and rode free.

Looking back, I can see just how little we had. One summer dad bought a six pack of Coke. That was a real treat. No, that is an understatement. It was the highlight of my day. There were four of us fishing and not enough for two each. Would you believe that dad actually let me have two bottles? I wonder how the others felt when they saw me downing the second.

Another holiday highlight was going to a moving picture. The hip term was "the movies". Once we took in two on the same day. Can you imagine that? Big deal, you say! Well, back then it was. It was big to go to a show and bigger still to have the money to do it.

This was a time when there was no money for the likes of an annual dental check-up. You usually didn't go until you had a "Jim dandy" toothache and then the solution was to yank it out. I can vaguely remember a discussion with my dad on the way to a dentist. "It'll cost two dollars son, three if he has to freeze it. What do you think? Can you handle it without?" I'd guess that I wasn't much older than ten at the time.

Of necessity I found work. I was a stable hand at the nearby dairy, cut grass, scooped ice cream, shoveled snow, hocked papers, cruised the meat counter at Loblaws, cleaned sewers, and for three summers, trained cadets. Of a truth I have never been out of work -- never.

I loved my job at Loblaws. Back in those days you still served customers on an individual basis. All meats were sold in the same manner as staff now operate a deli counter. Very soon you developed your own customers. People would often hold back until you were available to serve them. Those relationships were kind of special and they were often fun.

I loved it when someone purchased a turkey or chicken and asked me to "draw it" for them. Of course they meant for me to gut it but, if the relationship was right, I would draw them a bird on wrapping paper and present it to them. The usual reaction was laughter and a closer bond. When someone asked for a couple of dog bones, my response was, "We don't sell dogs ma'am. Would a beef bone do?"

"Oh, Mac (my nickname on the meat counter), you know what I mean."

Cleaning sewers was a great experience too. I was swing man on a crew of four for a summer. They each got two weeks holidays and I pinch hit for them in turn. None of them had even graduated from public school, but they taught me a lot about teamwork and about caring. They treated this kid really well. They never tried to use me. They even tried to teach me how to pace myself better, a lesson that I have not yet fully learned. One bonus of the job was that, on the way home, you never had a problem getting a seat on the bus!

Just to round out your awareness of the industry of my early life and to give you a glimpse of the passage of history, let me list a handful of other things. Part of my dairy experience each day included the delivery of milk by horse and wagon.

I also learned Morse Code -- you know: dots and dashes. I could send and receive at about 18 words a minute using what was called a key. The operation of a manual switchboard was numbered among my skills. If you visit the Bell Homestead in Brantford, Ontario, you can see a switchboard exactly like the one on which I worked.

I belonged to the "Over 99 Club". No, it wasn't an old folks' assembly, but a fraternity of marksmen. To be a member you had to shoot ten targets of ten rounds each and have a collective score of not less than 99. Obviously, this was a skill level that would enhance my military acumen.

Once I caddied at the Ontario Open, although my guy didn't win. Then there was the maintenance of a lawn bowling green in the experience mix, as was work in the distribution room of *The London Free Press*. In the latter, we had to add the weekend supplements into the papers by hand.

Keep in mind now that I did all these things as a kid. My experience on the farm included the stooking of sheaves, the milking of cows by hand and the thrashing of grain. The latter was done on a co-op basis as the team moved from farm to farm. That way each farmer was spared the expense of owning his own thrasher and hiring a huge crew.

In the old days, tires had inner tubes. Getting at them to make the repair was a very big, hands-on job. I've done it as part of my responsibilities when I worked at a service station pumping gas. Even in my day they had electric pumps, but not at all stations. At one place I hand pumped the requested quantity into a glass cylinder that was atop the mechanism. It was marked much like a measuring cup. Then it was gravity fed into the car.

I delivered newspapers for *The London Free Press* and the *Globe and Mail*. For the latter I got up at 3:30 a.m., met the truck coming in from Toronto, delivered as many as five routes and was in school by 8:55. In exchange for a free lunch, I served as cashier in our school cafeteria.

My father once ran for Alderman in London and I did door-to-door work to support that. He came in a very respectable third.

All of these were character building experiences and I am thankful for each one.

With frequent house moves, we often needed to search for a new church. If I could call any one home, it would be Central Baptist in London. Getting to Sunday School was a bit of a chore. We didn't own a car throughout my youth. Buses didn't start running until 10:30 a.m., so each Sunday I was faced with a route march of about three miles from home to Central. There I had the rewarding privilege of operating the projector for chorus time.

Then too, many of our moves meant new schools and the need to find my place in the order of things. Not infrequently, that was learned at the pointed end of a set of knuckles.

The fight that I remember best is one I got into defending my sister -- I think. As I recall, I was surrounded by a school yard full of strange faces, an impenetrable ring of kids. At first I was taking an awful beating. There was no avenue of escape, not that escaping was really an option. But then the tide changed.

We had moved in the early days of summer and, once we were settled in, I had gone in search of a new friend and found one. I can't for the life of me remember his name, but the reality of the depth to which our hearts had become linked was revealed that day in my ring of terror.

Somehow he worked his way through that mob and had the courage to begin cheering me on. One voice in the midst of a chorus of opposition. It made all the difference in the world! There was a new kid on the block and he wasn't one to be messed with!

Chapter 3
THE HALLS OF HIGHER LEARNING

The war came to an end in 1945. I was fourteen that year and about to receive one of the greatest thrills of my life. At Central Collegiate they had a Cadet Corps. We got a real uniform with badges and braid and all sorts of good stuff. You have no idea how proud I was to put on my first uniform! At last I was a soldier! I really couldn't understand why some guys were indifferent to the idea. For me it was a dream come true!

Year one: Cadet Private. Year two: Sergeant. Year three: Lieutenant. Year four: Major. Final year: Cadet Lieutenant-Colonel, Commanding Officer.

That year we won the Lord Strathconna Shield as the best Corps in Western Ontario. Hey! We were good! We put on a machine gun demonstration at our final inspection. One of the fellows, acting as the enemy, forgot to tell his mom that we were just using blanks. When he died so dramatically, she screamed and fainted. Somebody had shot her Johnny! Hey! We really were good!

In the fall of that year, there was a Corps church parade. It was a very big event and drew the support of the majority of the student body and many parents. As Commanding Officer, I was invited to read the Scripture. Oh, oh! You see, as a youngster I used to stutter and lisp quite badly. To help me my parents arranged elocution lessons, but I still did not read well out loud.

Needless to say I was more than a little concerned about messing up in front of my peers. So I began to read the text (Proverbs 3: 1-12) over and over until, on the day of the parade, I was able to recite it from memory. "My son, forget not my law; but let thine heart keep my commandments. For length of days, and long life, and peace, shall they add to thee

...Trust in the Lord with all thine heart; and lean not unto thine own understanding. In all thy ways acknowledge Him, and He shall direct thy paths..."

I can't remember a word that the Pastor spoke that Sunday, but I have never forgotten the Word of God. That portion has provided my life verses. I knew that I wasn't really living in accordance with the Word and I determined to do something about it. On January 23, 1951, at a Youth for Christ rally held in London, Ontario, I went forward to rededicate my life to the Lord Jesus. Incidentally, Barry Moore, who arguably became Canada's most renowned evangelist, counseled me that night and has prayed for me every Thursday since. Later he resurfaced in my life when I was commanding a real battalion.

High school was marked by many other special moments and activities. For a time I took voice lessons. My teacher, Mrs. Bishop, up and died shortly after she began working with me. Back then I bragged that it was my singing that did her in. Mind you, I don't think that is really true, because no one else died and back then I sang a lot, indeed still do.

I was part of our school presentation of *HMS Pinafore*, *Oklahoma* and a couple of major revues. Being one of *Pinafore*'s sailors was great fun and I played it to the hilt, if you'll pardon the pun. I loved to sing and when the occasion warranted it, with much enthusiasm. Would you believe that I actually gave a recital? Not bad for a guy who almost failed "triangle" in his kindergarten rhythm band! I enjoyed my Collegiate Glee Club and thank God for the opportunity to discover the majesty of the human voice. (Well, at least some voices.)

My enthusiastic spirit was usually carried forward into the classroom, the exception being my study of French. I learned my French with a Jewish accent! Doing badly, I elected to take the front seat immediately adjacent to Dr. Goldstick's desk. It seems to me that he frequently started the class standing by my side, his hand on my shoulder, urging my fellow students on in their studies. He would remark to the others that if they worked half as hard as "Monsieur Marsaw", they would be Rhodes Scholars. Then he'd give me a couple of pats on my shoulder and an affectionate "Keep it up, son." and he would leave me alone.

I left the class in late November, having calculated that if I did nothing else than translate the little book I had chosen from the library to meet that course obligation, I might just have it done by year's end. Needing to be sure of a credit, I fled to the study of History and topped my class on the mid-course exam.

"Spider" Webb responded to my enthusiasm in History by dubbing me "the General" (general nuisance, that is). His daily *Jeopardy* moments were a field day for me. My hand was always up first and I greeted any wrong answers from classmates with impatience. No, "disdain" would be more honest. In my first year of Algebra taught by an RCAF (Royal Canadian Air Force) veteran, my performance was so appalling that he suggested I get a pick and shovel and stop wasting his time. Five years later, as I helped with his grade nine tutorial classes, I reminded him of his remark. Somewhat defensively he said, "No, I didn't say that, did I?"

Miss McCann, my English teacher, marveled at why young gentlemen always chose the most gruesome Shakespearean lines for their memorization portions. I really couldn't justify my selection from Macbeth (rev. ed.) that included,
"...Better that I should have plucked the baby from my breast and bashed its head against the wall..."

Miss McCann, I really am sorry and I thank you for the tears you shed as you read from the grand old Bard. They helped me see the beauty of his work.

Business teacher Marjory McKee was a no-nonsense woman who ran a tight ship. If you were late for class, you'd find the door locked and had to go to the office for an admission slip. Her argument was that in industry tardiness usually resulted in being fired. "Mr. Marsaw" was one of her favorite "employees". Would you believe that she actually gave me 101% when I found an error in the exam she had created?

She and Mert Entwistle (who ran the Cadet Corps) were the two teachers that I was closest to. My wife Irene sent them our Christmas letter each year and, some months before their deaths, we went back to London to take them out to dinner.

I played a little basketball, a good game of tennis, some soccer and hockey, but nothing as part of a school team. At the end of my school day, I usually had work to do.

It was quite an honour when I was chosen to head up the ISCF (Inter-School Christian Fellowship). And, I like to think, I helped to elect Randy Lee as our school President in my final year at "dear old Central." He went on to become a fine doctor; I a fine soldier.

Chapter 4
THERE IS SOMETHING ABOUT A SOLDIER

A couple of years after I entered high school, I reached the ripe old age of sixteen. I was now far enough along in life to drive a car, even own one if I had the money and I could become a real soldier if I wanted to...and I wanted to!

In the fall of 1947 I marched myself down to Wolsley Barracks and enlisted in the Canadian Army's First Signal Regiment (Militia). There I was into such heady things as Jeeps, Harleys, radios that could reach South Africa, and war stories. I was rubbing shoulders with the guys who had been there, fellows I had longed to be with back in the war years.

I took to my new world like a duck takes to water. In less than three years I made Sergeant. With each successive promotion I had to get out the sewing kit and add one more stripe to my arm. But nothing ever matched that first one. From the perspective of the mature adult it might sound absurd, but back then I think I felt about as good as a medical student at the moment he is first called Doctor or a minor leaguer who has just been told to report to the Blue Jays baseball team. I was in the big leagues!

High school graduation came along soon enough. The future looked promising. The Mounties said they were interested in me and Loblaws offered me managerial training.

In the back of my mind, however, was the thought that if I was ever to really make something of myself I needed to go to university. That, frankly, was just about the last thing I wanted to do.

By June 1951, I was fed up with school and had no desire to sit in some musty old classroom studying whatever the learned profs would deem was best for my soul. Mom could sense my dilemma.

One day, seemingly out of the blue, she remarked, "Are you going to sit around here for the rest of your life? You've got to do something. Why don't you join the army?" So I did!

Of course her comment was not facetious. She knew of my love of the military and God used her to give me a little push in the direction that He surely wanted me to go. Ahead lay adventures that would provide me with a unique preparation for what would eventually be a second career (more about that later).

Incidentally, by the time I graduated from high school, war had broken out in Korea. Gaining entry to the regular army was, like so many of life's hurdles, a lot easier than it first appeared. Would you believe that Recruiting Officer Captain Jordan, RCR (Royal Canadian Regiment), urged me to apply for a commission?

"Become an Officer? You've got to be kidding! I know who runs the Army. It's the NCOs (non-commissioned Officers)."

You see, as a Cadet and young Militia soldier almost all of my close contacts had been with regular force NCOs and they were sharp. The Officers I most often came across usually were commissioned school teachers who didn't know how to wear a beret, polish a boot, or properly return a salute.

At the end of WW2, Canada's Army had been reduced from several Divisions to one Brigade. Regular Officers were a pretty scarce breed. Jordan's first job was to give me a close look at the real world of the mid-20th century Canadian soldier. He sent me on a tour of the local Battalion. There I got a closer look at the workings of a day in the life of an Infantry Unit as it trained for war.

What I saw led me to throw my hat into the ring. I made application to hold the Queen's Commission. *(If you haven't already read it, you need to. You can be sure that it will be*

26

hanging on the wall somewhere around our house. Just call before you come!)

There were three applicants the day I appeared before the Review Board: a WO1 (Chief Warrant Officer) with twenty odd years of service, a university undergraduate, and myself. The WO1 came out the room, paused just long enough to share that he wasn't accepted and moved on. They had convinced him that the transition from the highest non-commissioned rank to that of a lowly Officer Cadet was not really something he would find rewarding. Besides, the pay was about the same.

The university undergraduate was in and out in record time. He didn't pause to talk. He was obviously a pretty unhappy camper. He was swearing a blue streak and muttering something about the Board's lack of qualification to make such decisions. Needless to say, I found myself wondering what in the world I was doing there. If those guys weren't accepted, it was surely presumptuous of me to even apply.

I sat alone in the hallway not really knowing what to expect. The Officers who made up the Board were all strangers to me. I did know that one of them, the Chair, was a Colonel Mahoney who wore the highest medal for valour awarded in the Empire, the Victoria Cross. If nothing else good came of the day, I could at least say I was once in the same room as a VC winner.

The door opened and the recording secretary asked me to come in. There behind a long table stood three immaculately turned out Officers. The Colonel extended his hand to greet me and invited me to be seated.

They didn't ask me any questions, but rather simply indicated that they were delighted that I had applied and that they were confident that I would do well. My performance record and recommendations had obviously gone before me.

I was to report to Officer Candidate School (OCS) and, on completion of phase one, would be assigned to an Infantry Regiment. There I would begin my preparation for posting to Korea.

I was going to war!

Chapter 5
A SCHOOL OF ANOTHER KIND

Location? Camp Borden, just north of Toronto and west of Barrie. In my early years it was the home of both the Armour and the Infantry Corps Schools. During WW2, they were bustling enterprises. With the outbreak of the Korean fighting and the establishment of NATO (North Atlantic Treaty Organization), the feverish pace of those hectic years was renewed. The single story H Huts (named for their configuration) were still in pretty good condition, given that the big war had ended just five years before. They provided the living quarters and instruction rooms for the new generation of fighting men.

No musty classrooms. No pretty faces. No six hour days. Just the great outdoors, hard-driving instructors and work around the clock. The goal was to teach us the fundamentals of leadership and determine if we had the right stuff. It wouldn't be wrong to say they were out to break us -- to train us until we thought we were going to collapse, could go no further and yet had to. They wanted us to quit. Those that did got a first-class ticket back to mommy, no questions asked.

Officially our day ended at midnight but for most it began again just moments later. Almost as soon as the Orderly Sergeant passed through the barrack block, satisfying himself that all was well, the lights flicked back on and a new day began. There were weapons to be cleaned, assignments to complete, uniforms to be pressed, boots to be polished, "Etcetera, etcetera, etcetera." to quote a certain king. Nobody in his right mind would think of sleeping until all that stuff was done!

While they worked us hard they fed us well. Still, unusual was the trainee that exited from the Mess Hall without a sandwich or two tucked away in his combat jacket. Mobile canteens and coffee shops were not to be found along the way of a Platoon attack or an assault river crossing. They were very serious war games in which our infantry was to "close with" and destroy the enemy. We attacked physical features held by imaginary forces in every conceivable scenario.

What an experience those days proved to be! One of the trials they put us through was designed to test our emotional stability. In turn, each of us was led to a hole in the ground that was covered by a locked door and the test was explained. We were to drop into the hole dressed in full battle order, carrying our rifles, and then find our way out. There were several narrow passageways leading from the main chamber, each barely large enough for a man to squeeze through, but there was only one way out. Once you were in, the door was shut and locked. No lights. Are you ready to picture this?

The landing was a soft one because the chamber floor was covered with sand. On my hands and knees I began to feel around. There seemed to be five tunnels. The question was which one led to the exit? That shouldn't be too hard to find out. First check for any breeze. The through tunnel will likely have a flow of air. I drew a blank on that one. Well then stick your head into each hole and shout. The closed tunnels ought to sound different than the open one. Ah! Bingo! In no time flat I was through, back on the surface and feeling pretty proud.

A little time passed before my Platoon Commander called me over. He growled, "Are you in the habit of coming on training without the bolt in your rifle?"

"No, sir! Why do you ask?"

You see, I thought it was another part of the test. He was implying that the bolt of my weapon was missing and I was equally certain that it wasn't. I had put it in the weapon at the beginning of the training day. I was determined not to give him the slightest indication of any uncertainty on my part, so I did not even look down to check. Instead, I kept my eyes fixed on his. I was absolutely certain the bolt was in place.

"Are you really sure, Mister?"

"Yes, sir! Sure enough to bet a week's salary on it."

"Then what's this?" he demanded, bringing the bolt from behind his back and twirling it by its handle. It turned out that with the tunnels being so snug, the bolt had worked its way out while I was inching my way through. Fortunately it was found by the next fellow as he made his way along.

I never got a chance to read the report they put in on me that day, but it probably read: "No sign of claustrophobia. Bags of self confidence. Inclined to throw his money around."

Obstacle courses were a frequent fare. I remember one very special test. It was a rope that spanned the Cattawampus swamp. It was probably a hundred yards long. The Sergeant that was positioned to oversee it was from the Armour Corps. His job was to ensure that we didn't cheat. I was about half way across and doing very well when he called out to me.

"Where are you from Mister Marsaw?"

"London, Sergeant."

"What are the girls like in London?"

"Just fine, Sergeant. In fact, very nice."

"Not the ones I've met."

"I can understand that, Sergeant!"

"Drop, Mister!"

"Right here, Sergeant?"

"Right there!"

SPLASH!

Little did I know then that this was a precursor to times when I'd be up to my armpits in swamp ooze!

It was at OCS (Officer Candidate School) that I acquired the nickname that would stay with me throughout my entire military career. Here's how it happened. There were always two or three classes at the school during those Korean War years. Part of the assessment was one's participation in the program of entertainment which the new guys were required to put on for the seniors at their graduation.

I jumped in with both feet. Being somewhat of a communications expert, I organized a swami act in which the audience was invited to hold something up for everyone to see and then the blindfolded swami would, through his special powers, identify the object. A set of earphones hidden rather expertly under the swami's turban made the whole thing fairly easy to pull off.

From there the team moved right into singing "MacNamarra's Band." I was the fifth guy in what was billed as a quartet, and my role was to sing all the "boom booms" that are so essential to the successful rendering of that great old tune. From that day on I was "Boom Boom", or "Boom", or "Boomer". Those who really know me recognize that it is a handle that fits well.

Frankly, OCS was a picnic for me. Someone has said that the key to happiness in life is to find a job you really like to do, one so rewarding that you would gladly do it for nothing and then get paid for doing it. That's where I was at.

But there was one thing about it that was particularly sobering. At the end of my first month I was given a pay cheque. When I reflected upon it, I realized that it exceeded what my dear dad received and he was, at that point, a mechanic and a machinist with 20 plus years of experience.

Chapter 6
OF MICE AND MEN

Most people have seen a war movie. The characters probably were rough, tough, seasoned soldiers. The Commanders were beribboned and experienced. You can appreciate, therefore, the contrast I must have presented. Tall, skinny as a rail, with absolutely no claim to fame, I was probably the youngest guy making up the roster of the Platoon I was assigned to. You can't fault the men for questioning the wisdom of the powers that be. "This is our Platoon Commander? Thank God we've got ourselves a good Sergeant. All is not lost."

"Commander" and "command" are words that are not all that popular today. Most seem to resent authority. They don't like to be told what to do and like it even less when held accountable. In the Army, command is foundational to success. You command soldiers, often in action. The success of such enterprises depends in large part on how well the leader does his thing and how committedly his men follow.

My immediate need was to begin to win the confidence of the men who had been placed under my command. I think you can appreciate that that was no mean task. Beyond all the more obvious things, such as proving to them that I knew my stuff, that I cared about them and maybe, just maybe, that I was wise beyond my years, I decided to work at changing, to improve my image. So, I grew me a mustache! Now don't laugh. That wasn't the easiest thing in the world for a kid to do, I mean a young Officer. Hey it wasn't all that far back that I had first begun to shave regularly. Fortunately, I was past the peach fuzz stage so my early efforts met with some success. The results linger with me even to this day.

One of the many things in my early studies was the important matter of knowing the enemy. In this case it was the North Koreans and their Chinese allies. Some of our instruction included what to expect if one should ever be taken prisoner.

That eventually happened to one of the Officers with whom I was serving. Years later he talked about the endless brainwashing sessions he'd been forced to endure. His interrogators constantly harped on the evils of the Americans and of all the terrible things they were caught up in, germ warfare being one of the most heinous. He shared that, throughout it all, the maintenance of a sense of humour was critical to survival. One of the lighter moments of his captivity would eventually earn him a couple of hundred bucks from the *Reader's Digest*.

Here's how it unfolded. He and his fellow prisoners managed to catch a mouse. They made the little creature a jump smock and parachute and then hung it in a tree near the entrance to the propaganda emporium. Not surprisingly, the little fellow was discovered and became the focal point of the day's lesson on biological warfare. That mouse, as the Chinese saw it, was proof positive of the Yankees' diabolical works. "See! See! They are dropping diseased rodents into the North!"

In our studies we also learned that this enemy attacked in several waves. They sought to overwhelm the opposition by sheer numbers. It was pointed out that usually only the first of these waves was fully armed. The last two had to pick up the weapons and ammunition of those in the first waves, who were downed during the attack. The enemy showed little regard for the lives of its men!

The allies countered by including their defensive positions in the target list of their own guns. The infantry were to engage the enemy as long as they could but if the numbers became too great, they just hunkered down in their holes and called the artillery down on their own heads. They expected those on the surface would be killed; those in the holes would survive.

But for now, that's enough of my days with the Royal Canadian Regiment, where these thoughts were spawned. I was returned to the School of Infantry for advanced training. The rest went off to Korea without me.

Chapter 7
WILD BILL

"What's the Old Man up to now?"

"Beats me, but I can tell you that if you plan to cross the hall you had best be ready to hit the deck and roll, because he's sitting at the far end with his bow and arrows using the end wall for target practice."

When I first met Wild Bill Matthews, he was sporting the badges of The Queen's Own Rifles and the Princess Pats. He proved to be some CO! Those who had known him during the years of WW2 had called him the "Mad Shepherd." He had won not one but two Military Crosses for bravery. What an impact he was to have on my life, my career! As I see it, one of the true measures of greatness in this world is the capacity to inspire others to reach for and achieve excellence. That's how Bill influenced me. It was he who launched me on the way to regimental command. There is just no doubt about it.

Unlike my previous Commanding Officer, Colonel Bill was no stranger to his Officers, especially his junior Officers. He was a hands-on leader. I had only been at my new post for a matter of minutes before I was ushered into his office. He had already taken the time to scan my file and greeted me as "Boom".

"Where are you from?" he asked.

"London, sir."

"Hey, you're practically home." *(The camp was Ipperwash, just an hour's drive NW of London.)* They call this part of the province western Ontario don't they?" Without pausing for my response he went on. "That's great, because we need some good westerners in this outfit. You're going to command a Platoon in D Company. It's made up of fellows from Regina,

The Regina Rifles. That's a fine Regiment you know. They were the only guys in the whole of the Allied D-Day landing force to achieve their objective. They even went beyond and had to be hauled back. They've got a great reputation.

Oh, by the way, we've got a track and field meet on this afternoon, so you'd better unpack your running shoes. I'm sure the Company will be able to use you." And they did.

That afternoon I won the 100, 220, and 440. You see, all the practice I had keeping out of mom's reach really paid off. It didn't hurt either in the matter of winning the respect of those in my new command. There is something about working for the fastest guy in the Regiment. It was a great beginning for a relationship that has lasted a life time.

Coming to the Rifles had saved my career, for at this point I had begun to wonder if I had made the right choice. My previous post had been far too impersonal for my liking. As I saw things, a battalion ought to be family. After all, we were about to go to war, to live and maybe even die together. It seemed to me that the better we knew each other, the more likely we were to accomplish the former, the living bit.

The entire Brigade was directed to assemble at Wainwright, Alberta. There I set about soldiering with earnestness. The summer was spent in conditioning every day, marching several miles to different training areas and range practice, where we honed our weapons handling and sharpened our shooting skills. We also learned how to build defensive positions relating ground to terrain maps, patrol in the dead of night, treat wounds and injuries, and a host of other things that were part and parcel of a soldier's day -- living in field conditions and fighting the enemy we would soon be facing.

By the end of our summer training at Wainwright, my guys had done so well that we were selected to be the Demonstration Platoon at the Infantry Corps School. Our job was to show how to put tactical theory into practice, to put it on the ground so that others could see. What a team! My Platoon Sergeant was Moe Eager and together we led one of the most exciting bunch of soldiers the school had ever experienced! We know that, because they wanted to extend our posting.

Wild Bill said, "No. The Battalion is going to war and I want them back."

I'm not really certain what we had that set us apart, but I am sure that God had his hand in it. Right from the beginning, I tried to impress each of my soldiers with the fact that he was an important part of the team. I know they came to believe that. One of the ways I tried to communicate my respect for them was to deliberately avoid the four letter words that so many used to punctuate their orders. They soon learned that the absence of such flavouring, however, did not mean that I was any less serious about what I had to say.

No exposé on Wild Bill would be complete without at least one anecdote reflecting on his many eccentricities. If I were to entitle this little episode, I would probably call it "Traditions Are Made to be Broken." After a toast to the Queen, Wild Bill would take great delight in smashing his glass over the Regimental musket, which reposed on the table before him during Mess dinners.

On one occasion, the guest of honour was the Quartermaster General, who took the Colonel to task for destroying government property. Bill quickly assured him that the glass had been a cracked one.

A year or two later, the same gentleman was to pay a return visit. Orders went out from the Commanding Officer that the Mess Sergeant was to ensure that the CO's port glass was a cracked one. As the port was being passed, he immediately called this fact to the attention of his guest and in triumph, duly smashed the glass at the conclusion of the toast.

The next day the Mess Sergeant was advised that a new tradition had been born. Henceforth, the CO's glass was to be a cracked one.

"But sir..." the Mess Sergeant protested.

The Colonel raised his eyebrows. "No argument! A cracked glass, Sergeant Young!"

"But sir, I broke over three dozen getting the last one ready and, quite frankly, the Mess can't afford that."

Just for the record, it was in those days that we experienced Hurricane Hazel. You'll hear it mentioned from time to time, especially by people who lived through it. I think it has been dubbed the storm of that century. I came through it unscathed, which is more than you can say for my car. It lost its muffler climbing over some fallen trees. The hurricane did a lot of damage that surprised even me.

Chapter 8
AN OFFICER AND A GENTLEMAN

Somewhere in the midst of all this, my fellow OCS graduates and I were sent to the RMC (Royal Military College) in Kingston for something dubbed the "Couth Course". There was no debate over the fact that we were Officers, but many didn't measure up to the other half of our billing: the gentlemen part. That's right, we were to be Officers AND gentlemen.

"Good afternoon, gentlemen." said the RSM (Regimental Sergeant Major) who gave a sense of high expectation. "I have been selected to teach you how to eat properly. In front of each of you, you will find a set of cutlery laid out in the appropriate manner: forks on the left, knives on the right and so on. At a meal you always start with the outer utensil and work inwards." And on and on and on.

After a momentary pause for questions, he continued. "Good. We shall get down to the business of eating. Your meal will be served to you in a formal fashion, delivered from the right, with the unconsumed portion being recovered from the left. When you come to the main course, you will hold your fork in this manner, your knife thus wise. Unlike the uneducated riff raff to the south, in the process of eating you will not put down your knife and change your fork to the other hand. No indeed, you will feed yourself with your left hand. That will for a time slow the process, but once you develop the skill it will be seen that you will actually be able to eat more comfortably and, if need be, more quickly."

Of course we studied other things as well, like history and geography and writing, but you know all that stuff. Frankly, I think they were just thrown in to justify the couth bit. I mean, how could they haul us all the way to Kingston simply to teach us how to eat? (Although heaven knows some needed it badly.) As well, I'm not sure but I don't think that the RMC was all that well prepared for this adventure. It's unlikely that the young men to whom they normally catered would bowl cannon balls down the hallways -- well, not in their first week!

In later years I noted that the stacks of round ordinance (cannon balls) were welded together in pyramid-like piles. I'm not really sure whether or not we caused that, but I would like to think that just might have been the case.

It was during those days that I learned a lesson that was to influence my career. Almost every weekend I drove home to London. I was returning to Kingston in the wee small hours of Monday morning. In the town of Napanee I was hauled over by a cop for running a stop sign -- at least that's what he said. I think he was just lonely and wanted someone to talk to. However, what a significant conversation it turned out to be! He asked me where I was from, where I was going and what I did for a living. I told him that I was an Infantry Officer and he soon revealed that he had been a Sergeant during WW2.

The bottom line of this encounter? He said, "Throughout your career, you're going to have many young soldiers standing before you for some infraction. I'm letting you off this time, but when you're faced with those situations I've spoken about, don't ever forget that someone once gave you a break."

"Yes, Officer." And I never did forget! In fact, my trials became the topic of many conversations in the years ahead. I tended to do things differently. For example, a young soldier failed to show up for a particular responsibility and was brought before me on a charge of neglect of duty. His excuse was that his alarm had not gone off. I told him to get a new one and report to me the next day at the same time, with the clock in hand -- and don't be late!

When he arrived the next day I asked how much the new clock had cost. He reported $5.96 and presented the bill. He was surely a happy soldier when I decreed, "Well, young man, I fine you $5.96. March him out, Sergeant Major!"

Chapter 9

CAMP WAINWRIGHT

Our normal summers were, of course, not spent in the picturesque surroundings of historic Kingston, but sweating it out back at Camp Wainwright, Alberta. In my mind, it was the best training facility the Army had during my years in the service. There we really got down to training for war. As usual there is a host of remembrances.

Wainwright was a sprawling piece of rolling Alberta real estate, just chuck full of varying types of terrain. There was an area that rivaled the "bad lands" of the Dakotas, including a stretch that was honest-to-goodness desert! It was crossed by one river and a pretty substantial creek that, together with its surrounding swamp, created two challenging water crossings. Hence, these provided excellent training scenarios.

We had just been launched in a war game on what was called "an advance to contact". Ahead was an enemy -- their whereabouts not yet determined. Our job was to close with and destroy him. We weren't the point Company, so when we came across a Staghound (a large reconnaissance vehicle) that was stuck, I decided to see if we could help.

They'd been heading up the advance with all the enthusiasm that young soldiers can bring to such things, when they ran into a slit trench. They were a disappointed and frustrated lot. Although they had four-wheel drive and a really powerful engine, they couldn't extract themselves. Their front left wheel spun helplessly in the hole and their back right was high in the air. They couldn't get any traction.

To that point, I had no idea of the strength that was present in the backs of the 39 men who made up my Platoon. Of course, we didn't really have to lift the multi-tonned vehicle out of its hole. We just had to some way get the back right wheel down to earth. I was sure that once that was done, the Staghound would do the rest. No problem! All the heaviest guys clung to the right rear and the rest of us lifted the front left. Out she came! It was as easy as falling off a log.

The crew went away delighted and the Platoon proud. It was one more building block in the process of creating a fine team.

Now, on this particular day the force Commander had determined that we should learn what it was like to operate on a limited water supply. The heat was so intense that men began dropping like flies, so the Chief Medical Officer persuaded the boss that we needed a break or someone was going to die.

In the middle of the afternoon he ordered a two hour pause in the exercise for the troops to go for a swim and top up our canteens and Jerrycans. We were to maintain our operational footing while this was going on. My Platoon Sergeant took the first half of the guys and headed off.

Before he got back, however, word came down that the Platoon was to take up a position on the open flank of the Brigade and so, leaving my senior Corporal in charge, I immediately headed out for a reconnaissance of the site. There would be no swim for me and no water, at least not for the moment.

I had been told that the Recce Squadron was already covering the flank and that they would provide me with a measure of security. It was, therefore, no surprise to find one of their vehicles sitting on the very feature I was to occupy.

As I approached, they were busy scanning the landscape to their front. They did not see me coming up from the rear. I banged on the door to announce my arrival and to my surprise found that it was the same detachment that the Platoon had helped out earlier in the day.

"Hey, you guys don't happen to have any water do you?"

At the time I didn't realize it, but I looked filthy. One of the fellows disappeared for a moment and soon returned with an enormous washbasin filled with water. He suggested that I use it to clean myself up.

"Nuts," I said, "I'm going to drink it!"

I started about the position, determining the location for each weapon and trench. When sighting such things, it's necessary to do so at ground level. So, I would go to where I thought a weapon should be positioned, place my basin on the ground, stick my face into it for a good big drink, sight the weapon and then move on to the next spot, repeating the operation.

When I was finished, I returned the empty basin to its owners who broke out laughing at me. They hauled out a mirror so I could see myself. I looked like an old vaudeville black face performer, only in reverse. The part of my face that had been immersed with each drink was clean and white, with the rest as black as the face of a chimney sweep!

That summer we built a full Korean-type defensive position and then subjected it to an intensive bombardment with artillery, mortar and tank fire. The purpose was to prove to ourselves just how well a soldier could survive in a carefully prepared bunker or slit trench.

The bunkers had some pretty substantial pieces of timber built right into them and a roof that could take all but a direct hit and yet not collapse. The structure was blended into the surrounding terrain, so that it was not too easily sighted. Not actually being on the receiving end of the incoming fire, it was great fun watching all the fireworks, with bits and pieces flying every which way!

After about a half hour, the guns were lifted and we toured the position to survey the damage. The most convincing evidence of how well such defenses worked was found in the emergence of a rabbit from one of the slits. He was obviously very shaken and had problems hopping in a straight line, but he was very much alive!

In my later years, I began to make a list of the most unusual things for which people expressed thankfulness. If I had begun that earlier in my life, the list would have included the swarms of mosquitoes I encountered at Camp Wainwright. They were to provide me with a wonderful lesson in perseverance!

One night I was on a deep penetration patrol seeking to find a critical item of intelligence. The Commander planned to launch a dawn attack against the enemy's position and wanted as much information as possible about its defensive layout, including the location of any major anti-tank weapons.

I decided to approach the target area by wading through a swamp -- not the nicest environment, as first your boots and then your clothes saturate with cold, greasy mud and water. I had concluded that the enemy would never consider that avenue as a threat, so they wouldn't be watching it. My conclusion was right, but what I hadn't counted on was the impact of indifferent soldiering.

I was up to my armpits in the muck and moving according to plan, when over the back of the target feature came a soldier. He sat down only a few feet from me and lit a cigarette. You can be sure his actions were contrary to the intent of his Commander. I stood motionless. With every passing moment that became more difficult because I was surrounded by a swarm of mosquitoes that were having themselves a field day -- and I was their banquet!

Now, it was only an exercise and I might have been able to make an attempt at fending off my attackers. If unsuccessful, the worst thing that could have happened would have been my discovery. Sure, they might have taken me prisoner, but

I would have been delivered back to my own side in a matter of hours. But if it hadn't been a war game but a real war, discovery would have meant death. I decided to play it that way. I told myself that I must not move. It was a matter of life and death. Oh what I learned that night about the power of the will!

That year we spent two weeks in the mountains at Jasper. There we were not taught mountain climbing, but mountain walking. The Canadian sector in Korea would be quite mountainous, so it was determined that this preparation would be valuable. Mountains are potentially treacherous places and there is a way to move about them with relative safety. One can never know, but the training just might have saved some injuries and even lives.

As with other training, the purpose of this exercise was conditioning and, in the process, learning the skill of mountain walking. This type of walking is done as flat footed as possible, so as not to strain the lower body joints. The intimate presence of some of the world's most majestic terrain was, of course, the big bonus of the experience. At one point, we observed a magnificent rainbow, both ends of which came to earth only a few yards apart. No, there was no pot of gold!

Years later the dangers were brought home to me, when a good friend of mine died during his descent of Mt. Worthington. He had led an expedition up the mountain for a commemoration service, but on the way down he stepped on some rotten rock and plunged to his death.

There were two highlights of our time at Jasper. One was the presence of Marilyn Monroe and Robert Mitchem for the filming of "The River of No Return." Marilyn almost drowned during that little exercise! The other was to see, at the end of a two-day march up the water course of Nation Creek, one of my soldiers wade into the stream and catch a fish "bear style". He scooped one right out of the water with his bare hand – or should I say bear paw!

There was one particular physical feature at Jasper that was very much like those we were to encounter in Korea. We used it to practice the sighting of our defenses and the construction of our emplacements (bunkers and slit trenches). Let me explain what "sighting our defenses" is. It's the detailed positioning of each weapon to ensure blanket fields of fire and yet provide an adequate measure of concealment. Fire must be interlocking and mutually supporting, so as to provide a wall of bullets that blocks enemy movement and protects our troops. We also spent hours learning how to move against an enemy holding ground in the same manner.

One of the drills that we eagerly strove to work out was the capture of a prisoner. That took long, patient hours. It was good stuff!

At the completion of the summer training in 1953, we returned to Camp Ipperwash to train and wait out the last few months before our departure. Time was getting short. At breakfast one morning, the MO (Medical Officer) put in an appearance and sat down at our table. This hadn't happened before with someone of his rank, but everyone relaxed and there was good-humoured banter -- a lot of it!

"I can see you guys are in good spirits." he said. "Are you all as well as you look?"

After a very brief pause, he continued. "If you'll promise that you won't up and die on me in the next couple of months, I'm willing to clear you for Korean service. I assume you all want to go, don't you?" With that he grabbed a paper napkin, listed the names of all the fellows around the table and headed off.

As soon as he was out the door, someone remarked, "Gentlemen, I think we have all just had our predeployment medical."

He was right.

Chapter 10
OFF TO KOREA

After traveling across the nation by rail and then south to Seattle, Washington, we set sail for Korea on board the USS Marine Lynx, a vintage troop ship. Actually, we didn't sail at all. In fact, the only sail material on board was for a burial at sea – for wrapping bodies before dumping them overboard! The Lynx had an engine. In fact it had more than one, so we motored all the way. For that I am truly thankful, because even with that kind of power, it still took 21 days to cross the Pacific. Can you imagine how long it would have taken if we had depended on the wind? We might still be at sea. Why we might have even lost the war!

It was quite an experience! The troops were stacked in bunks four or five high, with sleeping spaces so limited that it was a struggle to even roll over. The Officers faired a little better. They were bunked in tiny cabins, four in each with one bathroom to share. Preplanning and timing were important!

We were just underway when the Captain imposed a water restriction. The ship's desalination plant wasn't working well, so showering was curtailed. Whoof!

I once heard that sea sickness is all in your head and if you kept busy there'd be no problem. So I volunteered to take the first shift of Duty Officer. It turned out to be my last.

It's hard to say whether it was the sea that got me or the smell of several hundred unwashed bodies, but was I sick! I had nineteen days of it. I was so sick that for a time I thought I would die. And then I began to fear that I wouldn't die. It was so bad that, at one point, I hoped that the Lynx would sink and thus bring an end to my misery.

At times like this real comradeship comes to the fore. My fellow Officers did everything they could to bring me through.

First they hung a chinagraph pencil on a string from the top of the mirror in the cabin I shared with three others. As the ship rocked to and fro, it traced the tilt back and forth across the mirror. Then they opened the port holes of their cabins and played "Battleship" by the hour. Lying on their backs in their bunks, they shouted the coordinates of their shots and hits back and forth. From time to time, you'd hear a groan as someone would call out, "You got my destroyer and it's going down!" Oh, yes, they brought me crackers and apples -- so I'd have something to throw up!

At least I was not alone in my affliction. The most renowned of those who shared in my misery was the Regimental mascot. He was a beautiful Great Dane, named Duce Horn after one of our Unit's symbols. He carried the honourary rank of Lance Corporal. During the voyage, he was secured towards the bow of the ship. Oh, he looked so miserable! He lost a lot of weight, but in the end he made it.

Before the end of our tour of duty in Korea, we learned that the USS Marine Lynx had been decommissioned. The rumour was that it had split in half and sank, which was the hope of those that had endured the deployment experience.

During his time in Korea, Duce Horn turned a lot of eyes. We concluded that many were thinking what a good meal he would make! In later years he went with the Unit to Germany, where he died in 1958.

We stopped in Japan for a day and then on to Inchon, Korea. The harbor at Inchon has the world's greatest tidal variation of all the major ports on planet earth. Cargo ships come in at high tide and are birthed in locks, unloaded and then re-launched, so to speak, on the next high tide.

We moved quickly from ship to rail and began our journey north toward the front. The train was pulled by a steam engine belching black soot. It hauled enough cars to accommodate the several hundred men who made up the Battalion. It wasn't plush, but a whole lot better than sitting in the back of a cargo truck, bumping along the roads leading to the front. It also gave us our first serious look at the Korean countryside.

The train had hardly begun to move, indeed we were just on the outskirts of Seoul, when we were brought to a sudden and grinding halt. Those that had not been seated at the moment were thrown about rather violently.

What in the world was going on and even more importantly what should we be doing about it? Was it a collision? Could we be under attack? Boy, that would be a fine kettle of fish. We had no weapons! We were to take over those of the Unit we were relieving. All sorts of things ran through our minds. An ambush, a broken engine, a blown bridge...?

In situations such as this, the real leaders come to the fore. One young Lance Corporal leaped from the train to engage our assailants in hand to hand combat and in the process broke his ankle. So much for his leadership potential!

As things turned out, his proved to be the only serious injury we had during the incident. The problem? A minor derailment.

In an hour or so, we reached the railhead and were greeted with incredible enthusiasm by the men of the Unit we were relieving. They were already on a train which began moving just as soon as we cleared the switch. Those guys were hanging out of the windows and doors, shouting and waving at us. One or two had managed to smuggle some beer on board and were obviously about to have themselves a "Jim dandy" party. I would doubt that the Canadians, who had the privilege of liberating the Dutch at the end of WW2, were more enthusiastically received!

But wait a minute. If we are here and they are here, who's holding the front? Is it possible that the enemy wouldn't know what was going on? Was there some sort of agreement with them not to attack at such times?

We soon learned how it had all been arranged, but the one suggested answer that brought the most laughs was that the Royals were so rowdy, the enemy was just happy to see them go. They were prepared to do anything they could to facilitate our arrival and settling in. You don't really want to hear the details. They aren't all that interesting.

Anyway, thus began my thirteen-month tour of duty in Korea.

Chapter 11
THE WAR THAT WASN'T

This chapter heading acknowledges the fact that the Korean conflict was never officially dubbed a war. It was a "police action". It lasted for a little over three years and proved to be far more brutal than the thirteen year conflict of the Vietnam War. The experience it was to bring to me proved to be both challenging and rewarding. I moved ahead professionally and spiritually. Let me start with something of the latter.

In the months before our departure from Canada, there were a lot of marriages. I'm still not sure of the motivation. Some guys had simply found the right gal. With others it might have been that they just didn't want to go to war, to face death without having had a wife and maybe a family. I certainly felt that there were those who entered into this precious life experience somewhat hastily. The consequence was that there were some shipwrecks. I must admit that I thought about marriage a lot. In those days a young woman named Ruth had been much on my heart. Indeed not going the marriage route sentenced me to the loneliest year of my life. Few days passed without me asking God for a wife.

However, not having someone special had one very positive consequence. It gave me time to focus on the Word of God in a way that I had never before experienced. For the first time I really read my Bible. Many off-duty hours were committed to doing just that and not only reading it, but memorizing significant portions. I reasoned that if I should ever have the misfortune to be taken prisoner, it is unlikely that I would be allowed to have a Bible, so I'd better do something serious about "hiding the Word in my heart." I also memorized several hymns and choruses so that I might be able to sing them in my captivity, should that occur in the battles that lay ahead.

Now let me say a little more about the fellows I was serving with. What a bunch of great guys we had in the Unit! Actually the word "characters" might be a more apt expression. Most of us had a label. Nicknames were usually linked to the event from which they were spawned or traits which the individual exemplified. To give you a taste of what I mean, let me list a handful and leave the rest to your imagination.

As you already know, the CO had his label. So too did the Company Commanders. One was dubbed "Stainless Steel" after a Dick Tracy incorruptible character of the day. Another was called "Rapid Robert" because his transmission always seemed to be stuck in high. "Rattle Snake" wasn't really vicious -- his bark was far worse than his bite, "Lumpy" by virtue of his take-off of Red Skelton's "Willy Lump Lump", "Awful" the trickster and "Salty" the ex-sailor were some of the junior Officers' names that I remember. The thing is -- we were all unique. Indeed, we had to be in order to survive. "Boom" or no Boom, I hope it was my relationship with the Lord that set me apart. The CO was a generous guy and sometimes bought the whole Mess a drink. On one occasion he called for thirty-seven beers (or whatever) and one Coke for "old Boomer" and slapped me on the back. He seemed to know and respect where I stood.

What an endless series of adventures Korea brought to the fore! Beyond being the Commander of an Infantry Platoon lay a host of other experiences. Every Unit in the Commonwealth had some Korean soldiers on establishment. On the books, they were to augment our fighting strength, but in reality they spent most of their energies doing domestic chores to make extra money to send home to support their families. Colonel Bill decided that he would use them as they were intended and thus formed them into an additional Rifle Company.

To command them, he selected the brightest, tallest Officers and NCOs, or maybe it was the tallest and brightest. Yes, yes, height must have been the factor, for I was one of those chosen. Maybe it was the others who were the brightest. Anyway, for a time I commanded a Platoon of Koreans.

Frankly, they thought we were all nuts, especially the night we had a Corps alert and had to rush from a Mess dinner to our battle positions, dressed in our ceremonial uniforms. Most of us seized the opportunity to scale the hills on which our positions were situated, with drawn swords, yelling like banshees. It was the best alert we had during the whole tour. Great fun!

One of the songs on the hit parade back in those years had the line "I was looking back to see if she was looking back at me." That was something of the character of the year we spent on the Korean peninsula. With our high powered binoculars, we could see the enemy across the valley floor, looking at us with their scopes. But in 1954 nary a shot was fired in anger. In fact we had more trouble with robbers from the south than the enemy from the north. Those guys were always trying to improve their lot by stealing from the relatively well-off Units of the UN Forces. It was hard to blame them much, given that life wasn't easy for them back in those days.

I remember once that, while we were on exercise behind the lines, a woman hung around our deployment area all night. For security reasons we kept a close watch on her, but she didn't seem to be doing anything inappropriate. Of course we recognized that she probably lived somewhere nearby.

In the early morning hours, as we were having breakfast on the reverse slope of our position, she approached us. She indicated that she wanted our Mess tins. We thought she'd waited up all night long to wash these things, in hopes of making a little money. Right? Wrong! When given the tins, she immediately sat down, took an old soup can and a little spatula-like stick out of her apron pocket and began putting the bacon rinds and egg yoke scrapings into her tin. It was going to be her breakfast! You can appreciate that that was far more inviting than the boiled grass that I later learned some often faced as their near daily fare. Oh yes, we gave her a couple of eggs that we had left. No doubt it was the focal point of a family feast that very day.

A further word on food. From time to time I was sent to Kimpo Airfield near Seoul to meet some incoming personage. When I did that I always took a bag lunch to give away. When driving through the Capital, I would stop beside different youngsters and give them a sandwich. More than once I saw the whole thing being jammed into a young mouth, mainly because food attracted other kids just as flies are drawn to honey. If it wasn't downed quickly, it was likely to be stolen!

Another example of the plight of the poor people arose when we were doing target practice on the UN range "Bullseye". As we moved into position to begin firing, we could see that the area of the stopbuts was swarming with people. At a distance, they looked like so many ants. What they were doing was salvaging the metal – the bullets that had passed through the targets and become imbedded in the earth behind.

They kept up their work until the very last minute. In fact, to get them off the range you had to fire rounds into the extreme left edge of the target area. Those closest to the point of impact would begin to move, but not everyone would. In a few moments you had to fire another burst to the left of the next group of salvagers to get them moving. Thus you shepherded them along and off. It was a kind of game in which everyone knew the rules and adhered to them quite religiously.

Another experience I will never forget took place in Pusan, a city on the southern tip of the country. While there I watched a coal train move slowly through town. You could see huge hunks of coal being turfed overboard from the cars. From time to time, the heads of those who were doing the thieving would appear just above the edge of the hoppers. I was astonished to see how young most of them seemed to be. They were just kids -- little kids! Their appearance drew the immediate fire of the shotgun guards who had been assigned to protect the cargo. As the guards worked their way along the train and got close to where the youngsters were, the kids would leap off and scurry away. Of course, on the ground were other kids who gathered up the contraband and hurried off. As the guards moved along the train in pursuit of one group, others would climb up the ladders of the cars that the guards had vacated and begin doing their thing again.

One last thought of this nature. Just before we left Korea, the Battalion took on the task of rebuilding the schools in a couple of the villages that were situated just in rear of our lines. They had been utterly destroyed during the fighting. As tensions eased, people began moving back into their homes and with them their kids. In fact, people had been farming the lands almost from the day we arrived. In some instances the paddy fields were actually forward of our depth positions. The two villages were Chin Mok Chong and Whash An Dong. Now, don't ask me how, nearly a half century after the fact, I can still remember the names. It's one of those things that has just never left me.

But getting back to the operational side of things, I'm sure you will be interested in learning of the occasion on which I was first wounded in action. Even though we weren't doing a lot of shooting at each other, both sides patrolled aggressively. At one point I was assigned a patrol dog team to go with me. These animals had been specially trained to recognize Koreans and/or Chinese by smell. *(Amazingly, in Vietnam bed bugs would be used for the same purpose of scenting the enemy.)*

The dogs responded in a similar way to a bird dog scenting a partridge. They would stop in their tracks and point. On any given night there were all sorts of wild life scurrying about. Fortunately, the dogs were taught to ignore other creatures; otherwise, their presence would make the whole matter a pretty scary affair.

Well now, on this particular night I was moving along with my patrol immediately behind the dog and his handler. The animal stopped, but I didn't notice and stepped on its paw.

Would you believe that it bit me? An Officer! I can still show you the scar if you care to see it! I put in for a Purple Heart, but the Americans said the wound didn't qualify. I bet if one of them had been bitten by a patrol dog, he would have gotten a Purple Heart!

From time to time the Brigade ran Junior NCO courses at the Battle School. For some reason the leaders withdrew the Units' compasses for this purpose and, as a consequence, I found myself on patrol without one. Wouldn't you know it, I got lost. Somehow we ended up right in the middle of a minefield! Now, there was a way to help out lost patrols. You could call in, tell them your plight and they would throw a searchlight beam up in the air. You would take a bearing on it and plot your route back. Great idea if one has a compass, but without one, it wasn't much good. Besides, I knew the general direction of our lines. What I wanted to know was how to get all of us out of the minefield without being killed!

A quiet prayer, "Lord, I need your help." Then I told my guys to fall in behind me, put their footsteps right in the very spot that I put mine and go very, very slowly. I was counting on the likelihood that my body weight wouldn't trigger anything big and hopeful that we wouldn't run into anything antipersonnel. To be very frank, I was more worried about the hard time my fellow Officers would give me if they found out about me getting lost, than I was about the prospect of dying. There is absolutely no truth to the child's saying, "Sticks and stones may break my bones, but words will never hurt me." Unkind words have always proven to cause the cruelest wounds.

One more patrol story. Many a young man has watched an engineer leaning from the cab of his locomotive and longed to be in his place. Others have seen a fire truck tearing down the road in response to an emergency and determined that one day they would be firemen. Well, that was a wee bit how our Unit Paymaster named Waldo Walker responded to his daily observations of the Infantry Officers he supported. Hearing of their adventures -- their "war stories" -- he secretly longed to be more than an observer. One day as we were speaking, I sensed this in him and asked if he would like to go with me on a patrol sometime. Well, his eyes lit up like a kid getting a new bike at Christmas. "You bet I would!" he exclaimed.

The day of the longed-for adventure came. In the briefing tent Waldo followed the remarks of the intelligence section with intensity. Quite naturally he was a little nervous about the whole thing. What broke the tension was my remark that I was taking one of my very best Corporals along with me and that, in view of the fact that pay day was only three days off, he had been charged with the responsibility of getting the Paymaster back in one piece. He roared with laughter. As we approached our departure time, we had a ton of fun putting on his facial camouflage. We did him up "real good".

One of the main reasons why Waldo was in the Pay Corps and not the Combat Arms was his eyesight (he wore a pair of pretty substantial glasses), which might have contributed to the event that marked this patrol as so special. He had been told to follow right behind the Corporal and do exactly what he did. Either he didn't see or he wasn't looking, but when the Corporal "went to ground", Waldo didn't notice and fell over him right into the muck of the paddy field! There was a muffled commotion as his bits and pieces went flying, but it all served to enhance the rewarding character of the whole adventure. Now he had a "war story" of his own!

Throughout the year, the CO kept giving me new learning experiences. At one point I was named to command the Battalion's Machine Gun Platoon. We were equipped with water-cooled Vickers. These medium machine guns, introduced in WW1 and used in WW2, were big and awkward but did the job. They were replaced with American 50s midway through the Korean war. As usual I tackled my new role with energy and enthusiasm. Looking back, I can imagine that my performance must have been greeted with mixed emotions.

During a training exercise -- and we were at that business almost continually -- my Platoon was moving in a column along a narrow trail that topped a flood control dike. It had very steep banks on either side and absolutely no place to pass. Several of my Jeeps were pulling trailers and that made backing up any distance impossible. Well, would you believe it? The second vehicle in the column broke down. What in the world do we do now? We were under orders to be in position just as quickly as possible. There really was no time to spare. I turned to my Platoon Sergeant and ordered him to have the guys push it over the side.

"Over the side? Are you serious? The Jeep? Sir!"

We were at war and to not reach my objective because of a broken down vehicle was just not good enough. Many a battle has turned on the basis of timely intervention. That's how I read it and that's how I played it. I never heard from the boss on the matter and if I had I would have come back with the remark that I was sure he would have done the same thing. There is a saying, "Silence gives consent." I took his silence as an endorsement of my decision.

The Artillery Unit had newly arrived and they were not yet in shape. This was their first operation and they were having a tough time keeping up. The rapid pace of things continued throughout the week. At one point we had run out of roads and were "man packing" in our weapons and ammunition. I reached a place where the CO was supposed to be and inquired of a Gunner (an Artillery private) if he'd seen him.

Then I spotted the Old Man and pointed him out by saying, "Ah! There's the CO."

The lad looked over and then came back with, "That's no CO! That's a bloody mountain goat!"

In all fairness, Colonel Bill set a pretty hectic pace.

Chapter 12
A LITTLE R & R

Sometime during the tour of duty, each of us was given a couple of weeks R & R. The initials stood for "rest and recreation", but the popular expression was "rack and ruin". Most took their time off in Japan and that was my choice. On the way, I met Americans Melvin Feldman and Rudy Thomas. They were Officers in the US Transportation Corps and we became good friends. The latter was a coloured man ("coloured" was the term used then for African-Americans). Looking back, I realize that he was my first "coloured" friend.

We had a wonderful time together. I decided I would return to Korea on the Americans' schedule, so we could maximize our time together. With that in mind, during my R & R I completed the regimental business which I'd been assigned, instead of taking an extra day or two to do so, as others had done. That decision had an influence on a later event.

Japan was fabulous. The highlight that pops into my mind is our rickshaw race. Rickshaws were the mode of transportation for many. It seemed to us that not to take a ride in one would be to miss a truly unique life experience. So, finding three unengaged vehicles sitting at the same corner, we each jumped into one. We hadn't gone far when someone suggested a race. The drivers didn't speak the language very well, but they picked up the idea and agreed to have a go. It suggested to me that we weren't the first to raise the idea and I dare say they anticipated a substantial tip.

Off we went, but it immediately became evident to me that my old guy wasn't going to do too well against the younger men who were hauling Melvin and Rudy. In a moment's time, I was well behind. I got my guy to stop, we switched places, and I took off! Surprise! My team won. I must have been in really good shape, which is more than I can say for my pen-pushing American friends.

Back in Korea, out of the blue the Second-in-Command called me into his office. "Boom, we noticed that when you went to Japan on R & R, you undertook to do the assigned regimental business within the period allotted for your personal use. You are the only Officer who chose to do that. As a consequence, you have been selected to lead a Canadian Honour Guard to Hong Kong. You would like to do that?" He went on to explain the details which I share below.

Those who know Canadian history will recall that, during WW2, our nation rushed two Battalions to Hong Kong to assist in the defense of the Colony. They arrived just in time to be soundly defeated by an overwhelming Japanese force and taken prisoner. Many, too, lost their lives. Those whose bodies were recovered are buried in the Commonwealth Cemetery at Saiwan Bay in Hong Kong.

Part way through my Regiment's tour of duty in Korea, the official opening of the facility was scheduled and the Queen's Own were tasked by Ottawa to send an honour guard to represent our country. The Canadian Destroyer HMCS Sioux was to provide the transportation.

Fortunately my remembrance of the miserable days spent crossing the Pacific had faded sufficiently into the deeper recesses of my mind that I was able to enter into the venture with exuberance. We boarded the Sioux and headed south, passing through the Straits of Quimoy en route. At the time, the US Seventh Fleet was blockading that piece of water because China was threatening to invade the Nationalist-held offshore islands. The Captain really poured the juice to the old girl and she went through sitting on her tail, so to speak -- at thirty-two knots, if memory hasn't failed me.

On this trip, I got to play helmsman for a time. It was every bit as much fun as driving a Centurion Tank would later prove to be. And if you're wondering about my penchant for sea sickness, "Yes, I got sick again, but this time it was worth it."

Chapter 13

GOT TIME FOR ONE MORE?

As the cease-fire held and negotiations moved ahead, our political masters began reducing the size of the British Commonwealth contribution to the UN Force. It moved from a Division to a Brigade and in the process, the Canadian Brigade was reduced to a Battalion, our Battalion. We, therefore, were to become the last fighting element to represent our nation.

These changes brought some new obligations for the Regiment. An ROK (Republic of Korea) Unit moved in to occupy the ground vacated by a departing Canadian Battalion and we were immediately obligated to establish liaison with them. The CO gave me that responsibility. On my initial visit it became abundantly evident that they were a very newly-formed outfit with some enormous holes in their equipment inventory. I raided our Ordinance Depot and did all I could to close the deficiency gap for them.

One of the most remarkable evidences of how badly off they were was revealed as I waited to speak with their CO in the anti-room of the Battalion Command Post. By the way, it was all underground. They took this hole business very seriously. Anyway, as I waited I noticed some men squatting in a hallway, each holding a pair of wires. In a few moments one of them jumped and let go. The fellow at the end of the row ran, grabbed the dropped wires, hooked them to the phone he was carrying and shouted into the mouth piece "Hi. Hi." or the likes. I learned that they had blown their switchboard and those fellows were pinch-hitting. Incoming calls sent an electrical impulse through the lines, shocked the one who was holding them and, well, you can figure out the rest. Talk about improvisation! That just has to win the prize.

Even the uneducated observer can appreciate the significance of our help. The way they sought to say thanks will, however, almost blow you out of the water.

One day the Korean Commander advised me that there were some very pretty Korean girls in the next room and that, as an expression of his gratitude, I could have any one of them as my mistress for the rest of the Unit's tour of duty! What a door of opportunity that was for a testimony!

I'm sure the Commander was surprised to find that my commitment to the teachings of Christ Jesus precluded me from going that route. To help him save face, I suggested that a couple of Korean wedding dolls would be a delightful compromise.

Closing out was an unsettling experience. Three times our Unit went through the preparation drill for going home and three times our tour was extended.

The Canadian Guards Battalion had reached Korea and taken over from another of our Units. At one point they had been designated to fill the role of an ongoing Canadian presence. When the political decision was made to first reduce the force and shortly thereafter to effect a complete pull-out, the military had to go back to the drawing board. The Queen's Own were occupying the ground that was the last to be held by the Canadians. There was little point in handing the operation over for just a few weeks. It was therefore decided that the experienced Unit would see it through to the end.

I'm not sure whether you are able to appreciate the disappointment the Guards felt. While the comparison might seem a bit wild, it would probably be a little like a bride being left at the altar. An operational theater of duty is what every soldier longs for. To have it denied at the last moment was a devastating blow. More Units arrived from Canada to take over and were turned around and sent back.

There is fierce pride within the ranks of every Combat Arms Unit. On the surface, we are inclined to give each other a hard time. We wrote and sang songs of that experience, like "The

Guards are Going Home." Another mentioned the RCDs (Royal Canadian Dragoons) who were to be the replacement Armoured Regiment. It went something like this.

"The RCDs came too,
To spend a pleasant summer.
They're going home to Mudder,
Now isn't that a bummer?"

On the other hand and more importantly, we were an incredibly effective team in action. The fighting arms included five Corps: Armoured, Artillery, Infantry, Engineers and Signals that worked effectively together to overcome the enemy.

There was also a moment of great tragedy. After dinner most hung around discussing the on-again, off-again frustrations. One fellow headed off to write his wife what he didn't know would be his last letter.

A while later, we realized that a fire had broken out in one of the Quonset huts the Officers slept in. There was a great rush to the scene and an effort made to enter the front door, but the heat was too intense. I ran to the back of the building which was not yet engulfed in flames.

Throwing open the back door, I ran in and found another Officer down, struggling to breathe in the dense smoke. Gathering him up in my arms, I carried him outside. He gulped fresh air into his starving lungs and slowly recovered.

Later we learned that the letter writer had fallen asleep, his blanket had fallen over the Aladdin stove used to heat the sleeping area and it had caught fire. Sadly, he died.

Eventually it was time to head back to Canada. What did the closing-out drill entail? Included were undergoing medicals, taking our final round of needles and pills, setting up to hand over all the bits and pieces that we were not taking back to Canada, the lining up of trucks, confirming the inventory of

Quartermaster supplies that the Americans would be taking off our hands, etc. Just the usual stuff. Then we headed south to catch our "ride home".

Transportation home was provided by the USS General Mann, a much larger ship than the USS Marine Lynx on which we had journeyed to Korea. My usual reaction to the sea notwithstanding, the trip was almost enjoyable.

As we reached Canadian soil, the dispersal of the Battalion on leave began almost immediately. Some fellows were from British Columbia and didn't need to board the troop train that was to take us east. As the rest moved across the country, our numbers dwindled until, on clearing Winnipeg and heading for Toronto, I was the senior Officer on board. We were to arrive in the Ontario Capital in the wee small hours and I had anticipated a quiet adieu to the soldiers who would detrain with me there.

It was about two in the morning when I was handed a wire by the conductor. It was a message from the Regimental Headquarters (Militia) in Toronto. It read,

> *"The Third will be on parade to welcome you home, including the Regimental Band. See you at 0400 hrs. JGK Strathy, Colonel of the Regiment."*

Nowadays travel by train is unusual for many people, such that most of my younger readers won't have been in Toronto's Union Station unless they have been on the *GO* train or passed through on their way to a game at the Rogers Centre. Consequently, it might be hard for some to imagine the sound of a thirty-piece marching band moving through the tunnels and rotunda of that great station. It was something else, that I can tell you, for I was there!

And oh, how we felt welcomed home!

Chapter 14
"HE WHO FINDS A WIFE, FINDS A GOOD THING"

Selection and maintenance of the aim is the first principle of war. It is also foundational to the accomplishment of any other meaningful goal of life. I came home from Korea with a determination to find a wife. I wanted someone to love, someone to share the flood of adventures that were my days.

You've heard that some marriages are made in heaven. I believe that God certainly orchestrated mine. It is interesting to know that the Bible teaches that each soul was known by Him before the foundation of the earth. That being so, it had to be known that Irene and I would one day marry, for it was only possible that we two could have the five girls that would make up our family. They too were known by Him from the beginning. I believe that what happened was surely under the direction of the Almighty.

Back in my home town with two months of holidays in hand, you would think that the stage was set for the accomplishment of my goal. It seemed to be just what the doctor ordered. Hey, there was bound to be someone out there that would be just right for me. Yet I soon found myself en route to Victoria's Camp Gordon Head without a single good prospect in sight, although I really worked at it.

I arrived there knowing it was to be a short stay. I had already been advised that my next posting would be Recruiting Officer in Vancouver. Undaunted by the failure of my holidays, I plunged back into "the battle" with renewed vigor. Knowing that the Executive Officer of HMCS Sioux lived in town and that he had an unmarried daughter, offered me some real hope. The Exec and I had become quite good friends in the time of our brief encounters. His daughter was a very nice young woman, yet she, as others before her, did not seem to be quite right for me. I did not, however, let my time in Victoria go to waste!

Knowing of my imminent departure to the mainland, I began to compile a list of potential dates in Vancouver. When a fellow Officer returned from a rewarding weekend in the big city, I was often able to persuade him to give me an address or phone number. That source, together with the names provided by the ladies I had dated in Victoria, sent me on my way with a fairly substantial list of hopefuls. On board the ferry I met a beautiful blonde. I penciled her in at the top of the list!

I arrived at the Officers' Mess, Jericho Beach, fairly late Friday night. You see, military postings usually take place AD (After Duty) of a given day. So I had left for Vancouver on a late ship at the conclusion of my day's work with the Battalion. I looked at my watch and concluded that it was probably too late to call for a Saturday date, but then I talked myself into calling. (Oh yes, I had already learned that the blonde wasn't available.)

"Hello, Mary? This is Boom Marsaw. Your cousin wrote you about me and mentioned I would be calling...You did get a letter? That's great! Look, it would be wonderful to get to meet you sometime...Yes...Well, I was even thinking of tomorrow evening if you are free...You're not?...Well, how about Sunday? Do you go to church somewhere and, if so, could I join you and perhaps we could have lunch together afterwards?... Great! Where and when can I pick you up?" *(I usually tried to take my dates to church early in a relationship. It provided an indicator of where they stood spiritually.)*

Well, it was a delightful first date with Mary and I came away with the promise of a second date on the next Saturday.

On Tuesday Mary called. She explained that she really wasn't free to go out with me Saturday or any other day because she had a steady date. The only reason she'd agreed to Sunday was that her cousin had said I was a really nice guy and asked her to help me get settled in. "But Boom, I have a close friend at the residence (a nurse in training) and if you'd like to meet her, I could ask if she is interested. Her name is Irene."

"Hmmm. A tall, dark and handsome soldier and a gentleman... with a mustache...a veteran of Korea, with the nickname of Boom...a nice guy...and you have to ask if I'm interested? Give me his phone number and I'll call him myself!" Okay, so that's not really the way it went when Mary spoke to Irene, but I'm writing this thing, so I can say pretty much what I want!

On Thursday I began a courtship that led to marriage fourteen months later. "Thursday?" you ask. "Wasn't it Saturday you'd planned for Mary?" Well, I didn't think that Saturday's plans would go all that well if we weren't just a little acquainted ahead of time. Besides, we both had Thursday off, so why waste time?

That night we went to a movie. The way we determined which movie was to give Irene her first real glimpse of what she was getting into. Neither of us knew what was on, so I had to buy a paper. A couple of minutes later our minds were made up. With the paper being in perfect condition, I called out as I had years ago as a paperboy, "Hey now, read all about it! Korean negotiations stalled; renewed hostilities feared. Paper here!" She didn't run, but she did think I was a wee bit nuts!

Irene was an Anglican, but when we first went to worship together it was to a Baptist Church. What are Baptists like? Take comfort in knowing they aren't all like me. No, No. Well, unlike the Anglican Church, some might clap their hands and on rare occasions they might take two offerings. On her first encounter, the latter did take place. If I remember correctly, the second offering was for some pressing missions need.

The soldier and his nurse were a happy couple! It seems that we spent every free moment together. God had heard my prayers and, within days of my arrival at this new posting, He had brought a wonderful young lady into my life. She was sure worth waiting for! It wasn't very far along in our relationship before the idea of marriage took root, but as you know, my soul was more than prepared.

I'm not sure of the occasion on which I first met Irene's parents -- perhaps Thanksgiving in the fall of 1955. What matters is the influence that meeting was to have on our relationship. Irene's dad was retired Royal Navy. He was one of those unfortunate souls to have been born early enough (1896) to make it into WW1 and yet be young enough to still be eligible for round two. Actually, he was commanding a mine sweeper in the English Channel in 1939, well before the outbreak of hostilities. During WW2, he had a ship sunk under him and obviously lived to tell the tale. Charles Weller was a quiet man. He had retired to an orchard in BC's Similkimeen Valley. His retirement was killing him. Caring for an orchard is very hard work!

His circumstance gave me a very interesting insight into the character of his wife, Irene's mom – a small, good-spirited soul. Being aware of her man's physical difficulties, she went about quietly doing everything she could to ease his burden. I came away realizing that if Irene was like her mom, and I was beginning to see that she was, then I was dating a gem!

By Christmas time I was back for a second look. What a warm and inviting thing is the setting of a happy family. We had a wonderful holiday together. Irene was dressed in a Japanese kimono when, on Christmas eve, she kissed me good night. She looked so good. That moment was the best gift I received that year. I hated to leave. There was just no doubt that I was in love with her! But this is not supposed to be a *Harlequin* romance. It's an autobiography, so I need to get on with it.

In July 1956, Irene and I were walking along Burrard Street in Vancouver when she broke the high heel on her shoe. I took her to one of those repair-it-while-you-wait places, left her shoeless in a little booth and went off to pick up an engagement ring. When I got back to the repair shop, I tried to slip the ring onto her finger, but she would have no part of it. Not romantic enough. But how many girls can say they got engaged in a shoe repair shop? She didn't buy my logic.

Later, parked in front of the Recruiting Office on Seymore St., I managed to close the deal. I've often said she was the best recruit I netted in my two years on the job. It was to be an "until death do us part" commitment just as God intended.

We were married on October 6, 1956, in the little Base Chapel. Certainly it had been a long time since it had been a place of regular worship. Our marriage probably was its last moment of splendor, given that it was subsequently turned into the gardener's shack!

Irene had yet to meet my family, so after our reception at the Officer's Mess, we headed east via the USA. The honeymoon was with compliments of the Army. I was scheduled to take my Lieutenant to Captain promotion exams at Borden and attend a two-week Recruiting Officer's course in Ottawa. The schedule of those things, plus my annual leave and traveling time, allowed us to stay in the east for a little over two months. Oh yes! I passed my exams with flying colours, although it would be four more years before I was actually promoted to Captain. Still, it was good to have them behind me. Now I could start working on my qualifications for Major.

By the time we reached Ottawa, Irene was not feeling all that well. "I'll bet you a nickel we're pregnant." And it was so. We were really excited. Our Elizabeth was on the way. She was born July 24, 1957, the first of five delightful girls which God would bless us with.

Now as you have read all this, you might have concluded that all I did during my days as a Recruiting Officer was to get me a wife. Well, that is just not true. As the only bachelor on the team, I drew most of the road stuff. I was often gone weeks at a time and frequently put in very long hours. It might surprise you, but this young Korean veteran was in pretty big demand. In one memorable experience, I flew out of Vancouver for Victoria before dawn one morning. I was to speak at a high school career day. On the plane the stewardess gave me a

Life magazine to read. In the center were several pages of photos, with a brief sketch of the people shown. They were the fatalities from the first American commercial aircraft to fall victim to an in-flight bombing. Meanwhile I was sitting where I could see the wing and engine through my window.

Suddenly there was an explosion in the right engine! A light from the cockpit went on and searched up and down. Apparently nothing unusual was spotted, so it went off again and I went back to reading of the dreadful air tragedy. Again there was an explosion! This time the light went on more quickly and searched with greater urgency. I thought to myself, *"It's only 18 miles across these straits. If I were the captain and concerned about my aircraft, I'd try to gain a little altitude."* At that moment, the captain fed the plane some more juice and we started ascending. I said to myself *"Quit thinking, Marsaw. Nothing is going to happen."* Nevertheless, I put away my *Life* magazine and took to reading the ditching instructions in the safety folder. Wouldn't a ditching at sea have made an interesting chapter in my memoirs? Regardless, we landed safely.

Our first home was a few blocks from Vancouver's famed Stanley Park and about the same distance from Irene's grandparents' residence. They were a grand old couple. Arthur Breithaupt had lost an eye when yet a young man. That had put an end to a promising career in the military. Subsequently, he joined the Diplomatic Corps and finished up his days as a Commissioner in Burma. It was there that Irene's mom had been born. The Commissioner and I hit it off well. He was very pleased that Irene had "found herself a soldier".

Back in the midst of our courtship, I had promised Irene that if she would marry me I would take her to Germany. That promise was fulfilled sooner than expected. My Battalion was assigned to Europe in 1957 and I had the good fortune to rejoin it before the departure. I was chosen to be part of the advance party, a group responsible for the reception and settling in of the main body when it reached its new station.

Several months passed before I next saw my wife and daughter. It seemed like an eternity, but just as suddenly as the separation had begun, it came to an end. There was Irene, passing a large picnic basket through the window of the train she had just arrived on. Peering wide-eyed over the edge was my little Bethy!

Irene arrived in Germany feeling a bit like royalty. She had arrived at the Dutch port of Rotterdam and disembarked in the early morning for the trip to the Brigade area. As the train moved through the city, its route was spontaneously lined by the Dutch people greeting its passage with warmth and enthusiasm. They knew it was a train filled with Canadian families and they were bent on once more saying, "Thank you Canada for liberating us from the tyranny of the Third Reich."

That evening we took up temporary residence in a three room apartment on the upper level of a village farm house. You see, there were not enough married quarters to go around and those most newly wed went on a waiting list. Needless to say, we just wanted to be together, so a fancy home was of little importance to us. The apartment had a "carefully coordinated decor". I think you could call it "Gutten Olde." Only one room was heated. There was a wee table-top fridge and a tiny oven for a small chicken or a hefty pork chop. On top were two burners. One of them actually worked! The tiny sink had only cold running water. On top of the kitchen table sat an antique laundry tub with a scrub board that seemed a little out of place because of its newness. I had purchased a baby buggy, which squeaked as you walked, but it did a good job of putting the baby to sleep. I guess if I were to sum it all up (from my male perspective), it was just about what every young bride could ever have hoped for in military quarters. Thus began Irene's adventure in regimental life.

When I first arrived, one of my jobs as Housing Officer was to scour the countryside in search of places like I've just described -- homes for our soldiers and their young families.

71

Fortunately, most of us moved into regular residences in a matter of a few months, while others took over the places we vacated. After a period of family separation, these places were usually viewed by the wives as their little castles. It was just so good to be together again!

During our time in Germany the role of the Belgian Army changed and that necessitated a major shift. The quarters they had occupied were given to Canadians and once they were furnished, we moved in. At first only the bare necessities were provided, but bit by bit other things arrived until in the end, they were very well set up. For a time it was a bit like Christmas. At the end of a day Irene often had a surprise for me. "Do you know what arrived this morning?"

Our next residence was a three-bedroom apartment on the second floor of a low rise. It was in that complex one winter day that Irene and wee Bethy were in the foyer. Beth, bundled up in her snowsuit, was tied to a rope so that she could play outside, but not reach the road. There were no fences.

After a bit she came to see what mommy was up to, while most of her rope was still outside. Suddenly she was yanked down on her bottom, out the door and through the snow. Irene tore after her, caught Beth up in her arms and rushed towards the end of the rope. There, a couple of lads had found the other end, thought it was a nice bit of loot, and were in the process of claiming it for themselves. One look at the charging "mother bear" and they ran!

At this time in life I still didn't think that I read well enough. This weakness, I was convinced, was going to cost me at some future point. I had better do something about it -- now. So each evening I read aloud to Irene. Wanting it to be as profitable as possible, you will appreciate my wisdom in choosing such literary gems as Rommel's *Infantry Attacks* and *The Rise and Fall of the Third Reich*. Don't laugh! It was a good education for her. And that's the story I'm sticking to!

Chapter 15
THE COLD WAR

The struggle for Europe, which the pundits dubbed the "Cold War", was to go on for forty years, 1949-1989. Its commencement gave birth to NATO. The Queen's Own was part of Canada's contribution to the Alliance's land-based forces. In the event of the outbreak of hostilities, our role was to delay the advance of the Warsaw Pact nations long enough to allow our political masters time to decide whether or not to launch a nuclear strike.

The Warsaw Pact armies were deemed to be vastly superior in numbers. The need to delay their advance was often debated. Some men were concerned about the well-being of their families and suggested that if hostilities broke out, their wives and kids would be their first concern. I remember arguing that the best way to ensure the families' well-being was for the enemy to face the fierce resistance that only we could provide. I share this with you, so you can glimpse the undercurrents that characterized these uneasy years.

Of all the roles I was assigned during my three years in Germany, the one that most impacted the big picture was that of Reconnaissance Officer. There were six of us in the Battalion. Our assignment, in the event of war, was to serve as "layback patrols". In the simplest terms, it meant we were to go underground, allow the enemy to pass by and then resurface behind its lines. Our task then was to locate its headquarters and nuclear delivery systems and report the locations by radio to our own forces, which would target their destruction. The sequence sounds simple, but the reality would be one of the most life-threatening scenarios possible. We trained with an intensity motivated by the hope of saving our very lives! The truth of the matter is that, the first time I played this role on exercise, I was "put in the bag" (captured) in a few hours! The second time was far more successful. I gained access to a monastery bell tower, a complex that was in time chosen as an enemy headquarters. If, as would likely occur in a real war, the place were to be destroyed by fire, I'm not at all sure how I would have survived, but *c'est la guerre!* (It's the war!).

The job that offered the most fun -- at least my kind of fun -- was that of Pioneer Platoon Commander. The guys that made up this small subunit were sort of junior engineers. We built light bridges, laid mines and booby traps, did minor construction and best of all, blew things up! Boom!

The term "booby trap" grew out of the fact that, in a real sense, they were devices that were triggered by a careless enemy (or booby) who in the process blew himself up or was inflicted with serious injuries. In my day, the traps were triggered in four ways: the pull of a wire, release of a wire, pressure on a detonator or release of pressure on it. The most sophisticated bridges were put together from prefab components and provided a single tread-way for troops to walk on. They also built rope bridges, the likes of which I describe later in this book.

One task was to ensure the destruction of any military equipment or infrastructure that might help the enemy, should we have to withdraw and leave some things behind. Broken-down vehicles were a case in point. To practice this task I persuaded someone, I can't remember who, to let us blow up his old car after his new one arrived. The old one was turned over to my Platoon Sergeant with my instruction that each man was to prepare a different component for destruction. One man would rig the engine block, another the transmission, still another the gear box and so on. After each charge was fixed, inspected and wired together, we pulled back about a thousand yards and closed the switch. The car went airborne! Whoopee!

The Canadian Brigade in Germany had a weekly newspaper called *The Beaver*. Jim Mitchell, a good friend of mine from the Rifles, was named Editor part way through our tour of duty. I became the Unit's Reporter and wrote a weekly column. That responsibility later led to the role of Public Relations Officer for the Regiment when, in 1960, we celebrated our 100th birthday. To mark the occasion, many soldiers went back to Normandy. Beginning on its beaches, we retraced the path that our Regiment had taken from its landing on June 6, 1944 until VE-Day (Victory in Europe Day). That happy moment had come while the Unit was poised on the Dutch-German border preparing to continue its advance.

As we moved through the French and Belgium countryside, we took the occasional side trip to visit WW1 battle sites. Included in these were Vimy and Ypres. Vimy Ridge, a piece of Canadian soil in the heart of the French Republic, was ceded to her to acknowledge the unsurpassed role our nation played in helping France during WW1. It might not have been the hardest fought or the most strategically significant battle of the war, but Vimy was the first exclusively Canadian victory. There is a sense that, at Vimy Ridge, Canada shed its colonial vestige and became a nation. Thousands of Europe's finest troops had tried to take that majestic and commanding feature -- tried and failed. What they could not do, the Canadian soldiers accomplished. And the world sat up and took notice.

At Ypres is the Mennen Gate, an arch that is larger than the Arc de Triomphe in Paris. Atop the gate rests a huge lion looking eastward toward what had been the enemy lines. It depicts the British Empire which came to the rescue of Belgium during the first World War. On its walls are the names of 250,000 men who fell in defense of that city, who have no known graves. 250,000! Every night since the end of the Great War, traffic is halted at the Gate and a brief sunset service is held in memory of their sacrifice. In 1960, we had the privilege of participating in that commemoration.

Dotted throughout the western European landscape are military cemeteries. Sometimes there are unbroken miles of them, for in the wars of Europe millions have died. No visit to the area would be complete without a walk among the grave stones that mark the passing of so many souls. The words recorded upon them often give one a glimpse of the pain of those whose loved ones' remains rest beneath. One epitaph that yet lingers in my heart read, "To all the world he was a soldier, but to me he was all the world."

In that year I first met Princess Alexandra, then Colonel-in-Chief of our Regiment. What a beautiful lady she is! Her picture hangs in our home to this day. Later in the same decade I was honoured to serve as the Princess' Aide-de-Camp, dressed in my formal military attire. I served as her personal guide and protector during her visit to British Columbia. As the Aide, you run interference when necessary and are the go-for guy when she needs anything. You confirm that everything is in place for any action she is expected to take, like ensuring her speech notes are on the dais ready for her, etc.

During these years we worked hard and we played hard. The biggest athletic success of the tour was winning the British Forces' Basketball Championship. The Queen's Own won first one year and placed second in another. I need to note that, until we reached the British Army finals, the toughest hurdle was defeating the other Canadian teams! Our center was Doug Palmer, a gifted athlete about 6'5". His dear wife Lou was a very talented lady with things like paintings and carvings. I'll never forget the kind presentation made to me at our season-ending team celebration. Coach Jim Mitchell did the honours. It was Lou's beautiful soap carving of a Hollywood Oscar. The guys had voted me "The Most Artistic at Taking a Dive." I'm sure my frequent trips to the foul line must have won us a game or two -- that and the wise direction that coach Jim gave in the huddles. "Don't forget! The key to success is to run hard, jump high and put the ball in the basket."

Our second child was born in Germany, but not without a little coaxing. We took rides over the bumpiest roads we could find, but nothing worked. You have to admit that the scheme showed better taste than the castor oil and Coke we tried with Bethy! Sharon had decided to come when she was ready and not a moment sooner. Then she came with a rush.

Sharon was born in the era of Thalidomide, a "wonder drug" developed in Germany, prescribed for morning sickness during pregnancy. Praise the Lord, it was Irene's determination that things should be just as natural as possible. She didn't want any part of a non-essential drug. It was years before we learned of the blessed consequence of that decision.

In the late 1990s, buried deep within *The Toronto Star* was an article about gross deformities of the unborn being caused by Thalidomide. Affected babies often entered the world with no arms or leg sections, and malformed hands. In the late 1950s, many such youngsters were born to the wives of men serving in Germany. Many of those children never returned home. Instead, they were fostered by the German Government as part of the settlement. Many were educated as translators for the Diplomatic Corps. Joy filled our hearts as the full significance of the story -- and what could have happened -- settled in. As we saw it, God had been faithful to His promise of protection, even when we didn't recognize our need of it.

When I first arrived in Germany, I ordered a Volkswagen Beetle. Delivery would take some time, so I purchased an old 1949 Mercedes to use until the Bug arrived. Would you believe that the Volkswagen cost only $1200? Mind you, the $3200 for a new Mercedes was way beyond our means. A Lieutenant's pay was pretty modest in those days.

As soon as the Bug arrived, we were on the move. Every spare moment and free Deutchmark were spent touring Europe. We loved Holland, especially a little family restaurant in Nijmegen that served the greatest rotisseried chicken. The waiter wore tails and, with a wonderful flourish, carved the bird right on one's own table. In Denmark, Danish pastries were great and Copenhagen's fair-like Tivoli Garden was a ton of fun! The Black Forest of Bavaria and the majesty of the Swiss Alps drew us to those places more than once. I'd have to say, though, that it was just wonderful to visit the cities and towns of Germany. What a beautiful country it is!

And what happiness we knew as we "beetled about" (couldn't resist the term) with wee Bethy resting comfortably in the natural crib built just behind the back seat and over the motor of our little car. Sometimes we took Frau Schnetka with us. She was a widow lady whom we hired to help Irene with chores. She loved to get out and about, and took good care of our child as we explored her wonderful land.

Have you heard of the "Dam Busters" or seen the movie? They were airmen, mostly British and Canadians who, during WW2, took on the task of destroying Germany's major hydro-electric installations. For those who like to know such things, they were Squadron 617, flying Lancaster bombers. During the war years my weekly radio fare had included *Calling L for Lanky* which dramatized the life of a Lancaster crew on operations over Europe. I never missed an episode!

I remember that the attacks were carried out at night. In the raids, they had to skip the explosives in on the water, so that they hit the dam at water level, sank down and exploded in depth, against the submerged structure. The height for dropping the ordinances was determined by lights mounted at angles in the front and rear of the aircraft. When the spotlights came together, the height was correct.

Most famous of the structures might be the Mohne Zee Dam at the head of the Ruhr Valley, Germany's industrial heartland. The other two principal targets were the Sorpe and the Eder. When the latter was blown, it created a tidal wave that ran for 250 miles/400 km! It was in the area of the Mohne that the Headquarters of the Canadian Brigade was situated -- upstream and on high ground, of course.

In the second year of our tour of duty, Europe had a severe drought. It was so bad that the water level behind the dam fell to the point that Allied aircraft, shot down during the initial efforts to blow up the structure, began to surface. I never did learn if the remains of the crews were found, but one would expect so. They would have been listed as missing in action, but now it was possible to bring closure. *(American submarine crews that never returned from assignment are listed as yet being "on patrol".)* It was expected to take five years for the lake to return to normal, but in the next twelve months it rained so much that the Mohne was back up by year's end. The dam has long since been restored, but if you stand downstream you can see the gap that was made, because the new masonry is a somewhat different colour from the original.

Back to Canada via the SS Homeric, a comfortable, modern, Greek cruise ship. What a cuisine it offered! I felt a little jealous at some of the exotic dishes the more "able sailors" of the Regiment could stomach. But what can one expect of a lad who was raised on peanut butter and jam and deemed Kraft dinner and tuna to be a special treat? At sea I had good days and bad, but even the notoriously rough waters in the Strait of Belle Isle weren't so bad that I couldn't enjoy the view.

In our 57 years of marriage and 26 residences (as I write this in 2013), there are few things that Irene has ever packed that didn't make it in one piece to their destination. Pretty good, eh? In fact, Irene is so good that she hasn't even managed to break things that she hoped to break. You know what I mean: that gift you suspect was a door prize at bingo, but was given with such fanfare that you fear hurting someone if it's not displayed. Are you with me? Want to swap?

By the last night out of Montreal I was feeling fit as a fiddle. It happened that evening that the young lady, who was responsible for keeping the passengers entertained, decided to throw a really big party. Surprise! I was well enough to join in. The highlight was musical hats. Our hostess produced an amazing collection of headgear. All but one taking part received a hat. Picture this, if you will. We are dressed in our Mess Kit (our finest uniform) which is now topped by a ridiculous chapeau. Moving slowly in a circle to music, each man took the hat off the fellow in front of him and put it on his own head, because the fellow behind him had stolen his hat. When the music stopped, the one with no hat was out. Then the hats were reduced by one and the music restarted.

The first moments were fairly calm, but as things progressed, they deteriorated. One fellow put his head through the top of a hat so the guy behind couldn't get it off. Another stuck a hat inside his jacket, so he'd have one when the music stopped. As the numbers grew smaller, bit by bit the hats were torn to shreds as different guys fought for possession. Two of them, one being the Padre, rolled on the floor in a fierce struggle for possession! The poor hostess was almost in tears. She pleaded with me for guidance.

"I'd guess this is the first time you've ever had an Infantry Regiment on board. This is the way they play. Stop worrying! Your party is a huge success. They are having the time of their lives! I just hope your budget includes hat replacement." Now wasn't that helpful?

I had boarded the ship in Europe as a Lieutenant and got off in Canada as a Captain. The Adjutant remarked that I could consider it as a battle field promotion in light of my gallant struggle with sea sickness and the battle of the musical hats! I think we were the last Unit to rotate by sea, presumably not because of the musical hats *sortie*. Those with later tours in Europe were flown there on RCAF Boeing 707s.

On the way west we visited London to see my parents. Mom wasn't at all well, but I was convinced that, as with many moms, there was nothing I could say that would persuade her to actually take better care of herself. Sadly, that was the last time I saw her before she passed on. She was only 52.

Chapter 16

HITTING THE BOOKS

The next three years were spent in Calgary, one with the Battalion and two on staff at The First Canadian Infantry Brigade Group (1CIBG). The highlights of those years were the births of two more daughters, Virginia and Beverley, the passing of my Captain to Major exams and being selected to attend Staff College in Kingston. In Calgary many of my fellow Officers and I dove into the books in preparation for writing the next level of promotion exams: Captain to Major. The powers that be offered all sorts of help and much encouragement, but the bottom line was a personal commitment to a long and gruelling study program. Not only was it demanding on me, but also on my family. Every moment studying was a moment denied to my wife and kids. If dear Irene got a dollar every time she had to shush the children or remind them that daddy was studying, she'd be a millionaire!

Our girls were really great and continued to be throughout my years in the service. They never gave us a serious problem. The frequent moves meant leaving good friends and then the struggle to make new ones, adjusting to new schools and cultures, etc., but they handled it all like real troopers. Of course there were tearful moments, but the comforting spirit of their great mom helped in difficult times. Today they can look back at the unique experiences they enjoyed camping across Canada, touring Europe, etc. The social skills they developed in relating to new people continue to be valuable.

In preparation for what I knew lay ahead, I wrote an extensive list of all the reasons why it was a good idea to hit the books. I included such things as being better able to provide for my family, promotion and personal satisfaction in my career, and the likelihood of leading better and living longer. Irene really liked that last one. Being an Army wife had more than its share of uneasy moments. Each time I got discouraged, I pulled out that list to remind myself of the worth of what I was doing. I really believe in the value of such lists and have often counseled others to follow suit, as it pertains to them.

As the time for exams drew near, the CO called all the would-be candidates in to help them evaluate their progress. While you could sit for the exams more than once, failure on the first try would almost surely be a huge roadblock on the path to really getting ahead. One by one the others dropped out of the race. When I finally got to see the Old Man, he seemed to be suggesting that I would be wise to do so too. Looking back now, I recognize that he was just seeking to test my resolve. I had up a good head of steam (a railwayman's expression for being ready to run) and was determined that nothing was going to stop me. I made it! The only disappointment was that other Officers missed the tide of opportunity -- others who were every bit as able as I. That hurt.

One of the things I did for our girls was make them an ice rink in our yard. Lots of folks came by to use it. Another project that our children really enjoyed were my trains. I had a modest HO gauge layout in my basement, modest because my studies didn't allow me time to really engage in the hobby. The girls' delight was to go downstairs, turn out the lights, and stage a head-on collision! It wasn't long before I gave the whole thing away. It was probably the wrong hobby for a family that was so busy and often on the move.

I remember the day that CO Big Dan Osborne called me in to announce that I had been named to attend Staff College in Australia. It was quite an honour to represent your nation at a foreign institution and even more so at the level of the Command and General Staff College. He was obviously pleased for me, but remarked that with a nose like mine, he couldn't figure out why it wasn't Tel Aviv!

As things turned out, I didn't go to Australia. I didn't ask why. Some politics might have been involved and I didn't want to get fussed about it. I deliberately didn't even check to see who went. Whoever it was, you can be sure that he was a fine professional. There were lots of them in the forces of my day. In due course I was off to our own College in Kingston.

There I got to rub shoulders with nearly ninety fellow Officers -- guys that I would serve with for the rest of my career. That meant that wherever I went, across Canada or around the world, there was almost always someone willing to point in the right direction or, in some way, open the right door. In two years you can build a lot of friendships.

One of the funniest events of those days surrounded the birth of Virginia. Irene and the Unit Signal Officer's wife, Bev Spencer, were expecting at the same time. He had to go on a training course and asked: if the birth should occur before he got back, would I be willing to get his wife to the hospital? No problem. This was going to be great fun! Just imagine if I got to take two different ladies in only hours apart. That ought to start the hospital buzzing! Bev expressed her regrets at spoiling my party. She and Irene were going to different hospitals.

Well, in the wee hours of the night, Bev called to say things were stirring. "Should I call a cab or are you able to come?"

"Hang on, I'll be there in a jiff." In the middle of the night with no traffic, I got her to the hospital in nothing flat and hung around for a few minutes to see if I could be of any help. A maternity nurse from the examining room said that they were down to one bed and that Bev had a little time yet. She asked if I could I run Bev down to General Hospital. They had beds available and were prepared to accept her. "The General? Sure! No problem!" That's where Irene is heading!

At the General, I made sure they wouldn't soon forget this flustered father-to-be. When asked for registration details, I told them to ask my wife -- I just couldn't think. Bev had a good laugh. She assured the nurse that I was always this way. "It's our third, yet he's never learned to handle it well."

Alas and alack, the best laid plans of mice and men! Irene went in the next day, but in the middle of the day, so my antics were for naught. But the plan had a twist I didn't expect. Irene ended up in the same room as a Naval Officer's wife, whose husband was out of town, so I took her home too!

Actually, as Virginia was making her grand entry into the world, I was playing golf. Looking back, I realize that was a bit insensitive, but in those days fathers weren't allowed in on the action and I wasn't one for pacing outside the delivery room. I knew that Irene would handle things well. It never crossed my mind that there could be complications.

Hearing that the baby had arrived, but not yet knowing if it was Ginny or Mike, I hurried to the hospital. Now it just so happened that on that day I had scored really well and was pretty excited about it. Rushing into Irene's room, I announced that I had just had a birdie and asked, "What did you have?" Oh, the things that loving wives put up with! Two years later to the very day, we were blessed with our fourth daughter, Beverley Colleen -- the best birthday present Ginny ever had!

My appointment at Brigade gave me lots of good staff experience. I was on the AQ (Administration and Quartermaster) side for the first time. As a consequence, I gained insight into personnel management and supply. There's an old saying that "an army moves on its stomach". I was learning how complicated it is to keep the front-line guys in the battle.

With every posting there usually was some sort of community responsibility. In Calgary the base Commander thought that if we didn't do something for the kids, we were letting them down, so I began a teen activity. With a couple of NCOs and their wives, we launched a twice-weekly night out. The games room had lots of stuff, but most teens just wanted to dance. Their quarters fed the Jukebox. A hundred or so kids can generate a lot of noise having a great time. I often went home with a great headache!

Chapter 17
FORT FRONTENAC

In my day, historic Kingston housed all of the Army's major learning institutions. It turned out everything from Officer Cadets to Commanding Generals. Staff College was the intermediate step in the operation. I deemed it a privilege to have been selected to attend. Just getting there was an essential hurdle on the path to Command and I had made it.

One didn't have to be there very long before the really bright lights were evident. I wasn't one of them. In academics I ran pretty much in the middle of the pack. Mind you, I had long known that my biggest asset was my capacity to put the rubber to the road. There were lots of Officers who were smarter, but only a few who could out soldier me. My time in Korea had demonstrated that. The CO gave me a number of rewarding challenges. For a short time I even commanded a Rifle Company as a Second Lieutenant.

The studies were wide ranging. We examined historic battles to determine their tactical lessons. We visited major military installations to gain an awareness of the hardware of modern war and an insight into current operational techniques. A Titan missile base and the Marines' Quantico Beach were among these. We did the operational planning involved in committing a major formation into battle and sustaining it. We war-gamed a joint land, sea and air operation. Throughout these, we played the roles of Formation Staff, Unit Commanders and Commanding Generals. We worked around the clock, produced every detail necessary for the execution of the real thing and, as far as possible, related it to the ground.

Each graduate had a personal career track. From my perspective, the worth of this privileged training is best measured by a review of the professional opportunities it opened to me. They were highlighted by my appointments to the operational staff of an American Brigade, the role of GSO2 (General Staff

Officer) of the First British Corps, the command of the Tactical Training Wing of the Combat Arms School with responsibility for qualifying Combat Team Commands for the fighting arms, the Military Doctrine cell of the Canadian Army, and -- most rewardingly -- the command of my Regiment.

I think it's appropriate to insert a historic footnote here. Some events in history are so significant that they are markers for the passage of time. It was in these days that John Fitzgerald Kennedy, President of the United States, was assassinated. We were devastated -- the more so because there were three Americans on course with us. It was as though there had been a death in the family.

At the conclusion of our time at College we had a huge celebration. Because some of the elements are repeated from course to course, we were forbidden to share any details concerning the gala. Now, 48 years later and not having heard of the lifting of that security restriction, I must limit myself to telling just one unclassified item. If you want in on the rest, you'll just have to join the Army!

In addition to Canadians, the student body included representatives from a number of allied nations, including one each from India and Pakistan. Although their nations were almost constantly at odds, these two men became best friends. As part of the concluding festivities, they put on their own skit. It played on two issues. First, Canada was amongst the United Nations' principal supporters and had in fact been on peacekeeping duty in Kashmir since the partition of India and Pakistan in the 1940s. Second, Canada had its own potentially explosive issue, the possible separation of Quebec.

Enlisting a few Canadians as extras, supposedly caught up in a civil war, they rushed onto the stage and positioned themselves between the opposing forces. As the Indian Officer appeared carrying a large UN flag, he shouted, "In the name of the United Nations, India and Pakistan cease fire!"

After a momentary pause, the Pakistani Officer leaped onto the stage with his UN flag, calling out as he did, "In the name of the United Nations, Pakistan and India cease fire!"

Then the two of them got into a heated debate over the order in which the declaration should be given: "India-Pakistan" or "Pakistan-India." As this was going on they began to beat each other with the UN flags. The skit concluded with the Canadians, having laid aside their differences, enthusiastically watching the peacekeepers fight. After all, it wasn't that their war couldn't wait, eh?

The irony of all this was that, in less than six months, I was part of a UN Peacekeeping Group sent to their countries to help sort out the Indo-Pakistani war of 1965. The two men were deployed on opposite sides of the line not more than a handful of miles apart. Both survived the strife.

Our time in Kingston was significant far beyond the professional development of yours truly. Here, for the first time in our marriage, we were able to settle in to a local church. LaSalle Park Baptist Church was a small home missions work. Here I finally slowed down long enough to be baptized. Irene joined me in this act of witness. The young Pastor was Clair Hofstetter. We built a wonderful friendship with him and gained some insight into what it takes to be a good Pastor.

Irene and I initiated and led programs for the younger set. It was the beginning of a ministry that occupied us for the better part of two decades. It was in this little church, on something the Pastor dubbed "Baptist Men's Sunday", that I preached my first message. I figured that either the Pastor needed a day off or he had an insight into my future that, at the time, I didn't know. All in all, it was a wonderful learning experience.

One of the truths that took root at that time was centered on the sovereignty of God. Many say that the greatest need of the church is revival. I have come to see that the important base is God consciousness. If we could just see the degree to which He lives and moves within the unfolding drama of our lives, it would be so rewarding that, I believe, revival would take care of itself. Many experiences have shown the goodness of God.

When we arrived in Kingston, we already knew the date we would be concluding our stay. Just about the last thing I wanted to do was buy a house, but we could find nothing to rent and had to do just that. The house was in the bedroom community of Amherstview, about ten miles from town. As a consequence, unlike the majority of others, we had the added burden of unloading a home prior to moving to our next posting. At that time, in order to not lose too much money on the deal, we tried to sell it ourselves. Some weeks passed and, having no concrete offer, it crossed my mind that we might be able to trade the house for a travel trailer.

As things worked out, we found a last minute buyer, so you would probably anticipate that we would have "x" dollars in our pocket, but not so. By this time, we'd fallen in love with the idea of trailering. What better way to move between postings? With a trailer, we could turn the moves into holidays and that's exactly what happened. The next 18 years of our family life was wonderfully enriched by its adventures in camping. Looking back, we can now give thanks for the circumstances that made it necessary for us to purchase a home. If that hadn't happened, we probably would not have bought a trailer and thus not have enjoyed so many precious family moments.

From Kingston I was transferred to Edmonton, where I spent only two months before I was on the move again. As I have already shared, it wasn't long before I was assigned to the peacekeeping mission on the Indian subcontinent. Of course for this one, Irene and the kids remained behind. I didn't know it before I left, but in Pakistan I would meet Zaman, a truly remarkable young man.

Chapter 18
ZAMAN

In the fading light of an early spring evening, a young man was making his way along a quiet street in the city of Lahore, Pakistan.

Although the atmosphere was still, he knew that Lahore was one of Pakistan's major cities with a good measure of sophistication. It had a race track where the UN established its Headquarters, a golf course and some very substantial buildings. It still had the semblance of its days under British rule, including a huge cathedral, a university and a college. Lahore was a bustling area only a few miles from the military front and opposite Amritsar, home of the Sikh peoples of India.

But tonight Zaman didn't really notice the city of which he was proud. In fact, he scarcely felt the wounds of battle that he had suffered that day in his quest to represent his country in the 1964 Tokyo Olympics. The excitement of victory fully eclipsed his discomfort. It would be different tomorrow, but tonight he just wanted to bask in the thrill of his win. He was the nation's best in his weight class. There were those who enjoyed the heavies slugging it out, but at his end of the spectrum it was the quickness of the boxers that was the key to winning and he was fast. At times his fists were almost a blur as they punished his opponent. What a night it had been!

Heading home, Zaman just wanted a little time on his own, a few moments to wind down. He had promised his family that he would be with them to celebrate very shortly. His wife had wanted to walk with him, but he said she was needed at the house to receive their guests.

Ahead on the street, Zaman could see several guys standing together at a corner. He didn't give them much thought but, as the gap between them closed, he began to pick up snippets of their conversation. They were talking about the fight.

They'd been at the trials and had seen his bout. He moved to pass them by, but in an instant he was surrounded. Very quickly he found himself lying on the ground, bleeding from knife wounds. His assailants were gone.

In time, Zaman's wounds healed. He learned that his attackers were friends of the one he had defeated on the day of the attack. Their expectation was that, with Zaman out of the way, their man would be named to the national team. Their determination? If their guy wasn't going, nobody was going.

It had been Thanksgiving weekend when I learned that I was going to Pakistan. Our family had just returned home from church and didn't even have our coats off, when the base Duty Officer rang the bell to announce the "good news". War had broken out between Pakistan and India and the United Nations had been called in to help sort out the mess.

The Army had a standby list for such emergency situations. A person would be on that list for a year at a stretch. Such individuals were specially prepared for a quick response. For example, they were always pre-medicated, with immunization always kept up to speed. But at the time of the summons, my name wasn't on that list! I wondered what was going on.

At the United Nations' request, General Bruce McDonald was to command the force. When he had been in a similar role on Cyprus, it had been next to impossible to provide him with a staff that could keep him happy. Not wanting to go through the same hassle on this new assignment, Ottawa checked out all the confidential reports General Bruce had written in recent years. Everyone he had ever said something nice about was on the receiving end of a call similar to mine!

Oh well, at least there ought to be a few good friends in that crew. In many ways, dispatching me was the easiest part of the deal. True, the holiday weekend complicated the matter because stores were closed, but the base staff pulled out all the stops and did what they could to help. I was most concerned about my family. I gave Irene a crash course in hooking up the travel trailer and changing tires. Unbeknown to me, early the next morning she slipped out to go through the tire changing routine again. She wanted to be sure she could do it on her own without me standing over her. It was a success.

She just got back in the house when the next door neighbour called, asking if she did oil changes too! My answer was that she would if she had to; she is quite a gal! I've often dubbed her my Quartermaster General. She runs a good ship!

That morning I scurried to the base medical center for my shots. That is always a happy experience -- or not! For the first time, I met the shot designed to protect against the plague. It really felt like the rat bit me. The sad story was that I had to go through it all again the next day. By the time I reached Ottawa for an operational briefing update about the political and military situation as it was known at that time, it was discovered that Edmonton's plague shots were stale dated. Roll up your other sleeve; we have to give you another bite!

I arrived at Karachi International Airport in the wee hours of the morning. The airfield was swarming with huge jets, aircraft from every corner of the globe. They were all belching out hot gases and the scream of their engines was deafening. The temperature on the field was still over 100 degrees Fahrenheit. In less than a day I had gone from the freezing weather of Edmonton to the frying climate of Pakistan.

Later that day I flew into Lahore and crawled into bed. Boy was I sick! I had just enough energy to roll out of my cot onto my knees to ask the Lord why He had sent me there. And I prayed for the well-being of my little family, who were half a world away. But as young men are wont to do, the next day I was on my feet again and en route to UN Headquarters. Guess who was driving the Jeep.

You probably guessed correctly. It was Zaman -- the same young man I spoke of above. I learned that he was a University undergraduate and the son of a wealthy trucker. As the political drama unfolded, he decided to set schooling aside for a time and get a job with the UN. He wanted in on the action!

After the niceties were over, I told him that I expected to be in his country for about a year and that I was a Christian. I asked if he were aware of any Christians in the city. Zaman did not answer my question, but instead said, "I'm a Muslim. I'm unhappy with my faith. I've bought a Bible. Will you help me?"

He then recounted the story of the knifing I told you about before. He pointed out that the Muslim faith was supposed to be a brotherhood. He said that if that's the way they treat a brother, he wanted no part of it.

Later, Zaman accepted Christ Jesus as his Saviour. But then the persecution started, that to me as an onlooker was most unnerving. He was disowned by his father. His wife was instructed to treat him as if he were dead. The poor guy was even denied access to his clothes. Those in the know tell me that the treatment of a convert is frequently worse than it was for Zaman. Mock funerals are not at all unusual and real ones not infrequent. After enough time for things to ease a little, his mother sneaked out of the house to bring him some of his personal effects. She risked at least a beating if caught!

Through it all, he showed remarkable insight into their scheme. There had been a cease fire arranged and withdrawal plans agreed to. Zaman said that his family saw that the end of the UN mandate was at hand, guessed that the Canadian Christian would soon be gone and, when that happened, they'd get their boy back.

"Believe me, I know what they are hoping to achieve. It won't work!" Zaman stated emphatically.

UNIPOM

United Nations India & Pakistan Observer Mission (UNIPOM) turned out to be the most successful UN operation in the history of the organization. We were in and out in under six months. By that time both sides were once again behind their original borders, boasting of their victories while busily licking their wounds. It was a hectic time, but one filled with a host of adventures. Let me share a few thoughts that I recall.

Remember the prayer you were taught as a child? "For what we are about to receive, may the Lord make us truly thankful." The first day I went on Pakistani troop rations, I prayed that with unparalleled earnestness. The food they presented looked like it had been put together from the remains of a dumpster bin at a local restaurant. Know what? I went back for seconds and I've been a fan of eastern foods ever since.

The same place that fed me so well also gave me one of the greatest challenges of my tour. The Pakistanies were holding the south-western bank of a river which, in that sector, separated the opposing forces. In the middle of the river was a large island under India's control. Communications to the island had been lost, the land line was cut and the radio had failed. At the moment of which I write, these Indian soldiers didn't know about the cease fire. Consequently, they were still taking pot-shots at the Pakistani side whenever they could.

It seemed that the easiest solution would be for the Indian Army to send someone to tell their fellows on the island to cease and desist. There was only one problem. The eastern approaches to the island were covered with Elephant Grass, named that due to its height, not because it was a favourite grazing ground for pachyderms. Because it was impossible to see what was passing through the grass, the usual approach was that each movement of the grass was greeted with a burst of machine-gun fire. Consequently, we couldn't persuade the Indians to approach their men on the island.

If the matter weren't resolved, it had the potential of escalating into something quite serious. I persuaded an Ethiopian Officer who was on our team to join me in a daring approach. To the front corners of a Jeep we secured two large UN flags. They were mounted on fairly substantial poles. Going upstream from the island, we managed to get the vehicle down the steep bank and into the river, which was wide but not that deep. Then, with him at the wheel and me standing on the passenger side waving frantically, we drove right down the middle of the river and up onto the island!

Would you believe that almost the first words we heard from the Commander of the little occupying force was "Tea, Sahib?" Both sides were incredibly hospitable. Right in the front lines soldiers would have a kettle boiling and tea would be offered. My Ethiopian friend thought that would be nice and accepted. I just about buried my elbow into his rib cage. "You're going to drink every drop of yours." I told him. "These guys have been isolated for days and they won't have fresh water. They are probably drinking right from the river." As I spoke, a soldier took a kettle over to a pool of surface water, cleared aside the stuff floating about and dipped in the kettle.

In spite of it all, when I finally got home and went through the most rigorous medical exam of my life, I came away with an absolutely clean bill of health.

Then there was the occasion, while working in the same general area, that I borrowed a horse from the Pakistani Frontier Guards in an attempt to investigate an incursion in a spot that was not accessible by Jeep. No problem? That's what you think!

I mounted the horse and got him going but couldn't get him stopped. I guess he just didn't understand the Pakistani word for "Whoa!" when spoken with a Canadian accent. He took off like a scared rabbit, ran in a huge circle and ended up paralleling the stockade wall that ran across the front of the establishment. The beast was on auto-pilot! Approaching the main gate at the speed we were going, there was no way we could turn in! Wrong again! Like a clip out of a Warner Brothers' cartoon, he banked for a turn to the right and, with hooves fanning the air, entered the stockade and stopped.

"Good Boy!" said I while dismounting. "He's a fine animal, but I don't think my idea is going to work. We're having a little communication problem. His English isn't good you know."

Horses weren't the only ones with whom we had trouble communicating. The official language of the mission was English but, for over half of those with whom we served, it was not their native tongue. There were interesting complications.

For example, the word "right" presented all sorts of difficulty. Which is the right "right": a right turn, you've got it, it's understood, they have a right, right in line, right angle, right the moral good...? Then there's "write" as in putting pen to paper and "rite" the formal practice. We did manage to get one thing RIGHT. We started to use the Spanish word *correcto* meaning "right on". It was fun to hear the Canadians belt out "Correcto, correcto!" with great gusto. The practice also endeared us to the Spanish speakers. They thought the Canadians were a great "boonch". They sure got that right!

I have never been so proud to be Canadian in all my life! From top to bottom our guys did an absolutely first class job. Officers who back home were dispensers of fuel and counters of tent pegs were the kingpins in the operation of most of the observer posts. They drove vehicles by day and maintained them by night. They authored most of the station reports and carried the lion's share of the local negotiations.

Now, it might sound strange, but I'd have to say that the Indo-Pakistani conflict had the largest military show of my career: a Divisional artillery firefight. I was the Duty Officer that night when reports started to come in from our forward observers.

"All hell has broken out up here. They are pounding the place to pieces." A call to the UN Headquarters on the Indian side confirmed that they were experiencing the same.

This sort of thing always followed a similar pattern. It was the other guy who started it and neither side would stop until the other called a halt first. However, something unique about this outbreak struck me almost immediately. All of the rounds from the Artillery Units of both sides were falling in their opponent's infantry lines. There appeared to be no counter-battery fire. What do I mean? Well, the best way to stop the heavy guns from firing is to make the gun positions uninhabitable. The opposing artillery positions were not receiving any such fire. Both sides were going after the other's infantry, like a reveler shooting ducks at a fair.

I thought to myself, I bet those Artillery Commanders are good friends. They probably went to school together and were both trained under the British. I called the Chiefs of Staff of both Divisions, listened to their stories and then accused them of playing games. I told them of my suspicion in regard to relationships and ordered them to stop. I hit the nail right on the head! The shooting waned and finally stopped. Ah...!

We were there over Christmas. General Bruce had the bright idea of flying into all our observer posts with appropriate gifts, goodies and greetings. "Get me a Santa Claus suit, Boom. It's going to be great fun!" As the time drew nearer, however, he got cold feet. We were still going, but he wouldn't wear the outfit. "Boom! You'd make a great Santa! Ho, Ho, Ho!"

In addition to what Santa was taking to the UN observers, he/I took a huge satchel filled with candy. My plan was to grab a Jeep at each stop, drive into the nearby town and give the kids a treat that many of them might never have had. At the first stop, my full-costumed Santa appearance sent all the kids diving for cover. The red suit absolutely terrified them! Back to the aircraft for a quick change and into town for another try.

This time they approached with ease, but wouldn't take the candy. The driver and I each popped one into our mouths and attempted to communicate how good they were. Finally one brave little guy came forward. Everyone watched as he unwrapped the goodie. Into his mouth it went and then, a joyous endorsement. In an instant we were swarmed!

In Pakistan I experienced two of the three forced landings that happened during my career. The worst took place when an oil seal broke in the engine and completely blinded the pilot. To compound the difficulty, we were going into an airstrip that we had never seen before. It was an old WW2 airfield that had been piled high with rocks to prevent its use. The Indian Divisional Commander had agreed to clear just enough room to land. Jimmy Dyer, an exceptional airman, was piloting the single engine Otter. On the side of the plane he had painted "Dyer Emergency Airways." His words were too prophetic!

While he handled the controls, I tried to navigate from a back window. Once we found the field, we circled and circled until I became really familiar with the terrain. I needed to get him centered on the landing area and tell him when to set it down. To do this, I sought to identify trees or bushes that were opposite the start and finish of the safe area and then I had to judge when we were close enough to the ground for him to cut the power. Needless to say it worked, although I have to admit that we really bounced when I misjudged the height!

On another flight with Jim, I gained a special insight into the "goad" which is spoken of in the Bible. It's a stick used to prod animals to greater effort. Now, traveling by ox cart is common on the Indian subcontinent.

This day we were sitting at the end of a dirt airstrip ready for take-off, when an ox cart started to make its way across. There actually was a dirt trail that bisected the air field! The driver was dozing. Sometimes drivers fall asleep on a long journey. Oxen move but oh so slowly. Actually, we had lots of room to get off the ground long before we got anywhere near the cart. We knew that, but the ox cart driver didn't. He was startled to consciousness by the roar of our engine and spurred into action by the sight of the plane bearing down on him. There before my eyes was the goad in action. In an instant he had his ox sprinting at a pace that would have given Donavan Bailey a run for his money.

Jim held the plane on the ground just a little longer than necessary so that our wheels passed only a few feet above the head of the driver. Do you think he ever slept again? I have my doubts -- certainly not in his ox cart!

I simply have to tell you of visiting the Sunshine School, an institute for the blind in Lahore. The General had sent me out to look for something the mission could contribute to in the way of a humanitarian enterprise and the school is what I chose. The day I visited, the kids were playing Cricket. Now if there were some way to do it, I would love to stop right here and offer a prize for the first correct submission detailing how blind kids play Cricket, a game that's very popular in Pakistan. That not being practical, let me share what I observed.

The wickets were 45 gallon drums: one empty and one full. Behind them stood beaters who, during play, hit their drums to provide the players with direction. One was high pitched, the other low. The ball was metallic and filled with shot, so it rattled as it moved. It was rolled by the pitcher toward the sound of the drum at the end where the batsman was standing. Hearing the ball approaching, the batsman swung at ground level. If the ball got past him and hit the drum, he was out. If he hit it, he would run towards the sound of the other drum. Meanwhile, the defense had to pick up the rolling ball and get it into one of the drums. If they did that when the batsman was in between the drums, he was out. Going back and forth between the drums was the way the player scored runs. The game required the aid of one sighted person who, if the ball stopped, would kick it so the children could locate it.

As I watched the play, I was struck by the incredible courage of these children. They went flat out and on occasion collided with each other, though not often. Their acute sense of hearing gave them an awareness of how close they were to other runners and generated caution. I found myself just a little tearful as I reflected on the spirit those kids evidenced.

As I've moved through life, I've become more and more convinced of the truth that the Lord is "Master of circumstance". These next incidents are amazing testimonies to that fact. In my first week in Lahore, I visited the city's Cathedral, with its pulpit and Pastor high above the people and a reedy old sound system. It lacked the warmth I sought in a church. So, you will appreciate the happiness I felt when I discovered Forman Christian College a few days later. There was a small chapel on campus. It was great to discover a group of believers with like conviction.

On the very first Sunday at the college chapel, there was a visiting missionary. At the after-service fellowship, I learned that she had served in Japan for a couple of decades. I shared with her that my mom had corresponded with a lady in Japan for years. Did I know her name? Sure! It was Birdie Taylor. How could I forget? She used to send me stamps for my collection and I'd send her *Thank You* notes.

"Birdie!" she exclaimed. "We were partners for years!" Some would say that it's a small world, but I prefer to think of it in terms of there being a big God.

Earlier I shared with you about setting up a children's program at our church in Kingston. At one meeting we were privileged to have Dr. Howard Searle in attendance. He was a gifted surgeon who was going to India to serve in a Christian hospital. The boys in the club decided to adopt him as their missionary and, on invitation, he journeyed from Toronto to share his calling. Howard and I hit it off immediately. We agreed that the weekend had been far too short and as we bid each other farewell, we promised to get together when he returned on furlough in a few years.

All of a sudden I was in Pakistan and Howard was in India, only a few air miles away. In the lull between the signing of the withdrawal agreement and the carrying out of the operation, the staff were able to take a week off to do a little sightseeing. I decided to visit the good doctor and wrote him a letter seeking his agreement. I sent it across the line by UN courier and asked the guys on the Indian side to drop it in the mail which they did -- but with no stamp on it, as I'd learn later. By the time my break period came I hadn't heard back, so I decided to just go and let the Lord work out the details.

In those days, scarcely a week went by without a report of another Air India passenger plane crash, so there was a little uneasiness about the whole enterprise. As I watched the Falker Friendship land at the Amritsar Airport, I reasoned that if it could fly in safely, it could fly out. In no time, we were in New Delhi, for a two-hour layover. I decided to just wander around to see what I could see and actually entered an Air India maintenance hangar. There was no evident security. If I'd been a Pakistani agent I could have had a field day, but with what was going on, who needed an agent?

Swinging in the rafters were monkeys who migrated back and forth each year through the nation's capital. The maintenance crews worked under specially rigged sheets of canvas. You see, as the beasts monkeyed around (sorry -- it was such an enticing expression that I couldn't resist), they would from time to time swoop down, pick up bits and pieces and return to their high perches. When they got bored with whatever was in hand, they just let go. Thus the need for the protective canvases. I suspect that more than one aircraft was downed because of this monkey business!

Later that same day it was off to Nagpur and, as the Lord would have it, Howard was at the airport to meet me. It was at that point, of course, that I learned about the letter and its lack of a stamp. We rejoiced in how it had all worked out!

My days at the hospital were wonderfully enlightening. I got a white coat from Howard and sat in on the clinic's sick call and joined him on rounds. There was a parade of exotic maladies. Elephantiasis is the one that lingers with me. There was a little guy suffering from a terrible infection caused by the village medicine man's treatment of his severe burns by applying cow dung. The boy had also come in with a bit of "witchcrackery" around his neck. Before Howard would treat him, he insisted that the parents cut away the necklace. It was important that healing not be credited to black magic.

The medical team's day was long and demanding. There was little time for Howard or his wife Marilyn to do much hosting, so their eldest daughter Christie took over that task. She was a young lady about the same age as our eldest. She hauled me all over the place! We had a great time. I'll never forget the taxi line. There must have been a dozen or so beautifully-kept Model A Fords sitting side by side waiting for customers. I don't know how old they were. I'd guess that the Ford Motor Company might have sold India the dyes and the cars were turned out on an assembly line somewhere in the nation.

On my way home I visited the Taj Mahal. The Agra Express, one of India's fanciest trains, plied the run between Delhi and Agra where the Taj Mahal is. I took the first train out in the morning and found myself whizzing along at the hour when the nation awakens to its new day. It was the time for one's personal ablutions. The railway right of way offered people a small measure of privacy from their neighbours; however, from the comfort of my speeding train, I fell unwittingly privy to some very personal moments. "Oh, excuse me ma'am."

What a magnificent structure the Taj Mahal is! Let me share just a couple of remembrances. At each corner of the building, but separated from it, were towers. They were constructed on a slight angle, so that if they were subjected to a severe earthquake, they would fall outwards and not damage the main building. At the time of my visit, couples weren't allowed to climb up on their own because some lovers had used the site to leap off and die together. The story at least added a romantic touch to the tour. The main entrance was a towering structure that had lettering (words) that started at ground level. Moving upwards, the letters gradually enlarged so that at the top they were just as readable as at the bottom. There were two enclosed tombs. One was on the upper level for tourists to peruse. The one on the lower level contained the body of a key person and could only be viewed from afar.

I also had a few moments to look over the capital itself. It was the day before Prime Minister Shastri's funeral. He had died of a heart attack in Tashkent, Russia, while negotiating the end of the war with Pakistan. The city was alive with preparations. Even in its usual decor it is a fabulous place to behold, but in preparation for a special event, brilliant colours festooned every nook and cranny.

I also had a glimpse of vigilante justice. At the Zoo a pickpocket got caught. Justice was administered right there with a vengeance. The man was severely beaten. Even little children were encouraged to share in the kicking. After the people were satisfied, what was left of him was turned over to the police who had taken their time getting involved.

Back on duty, I spent many of the final hours before realignment took place, just "flying the front" (moving along the irregular line that separated the forward elements of the two Armies). The hope was that we might head off any last minute troubles. The opposing forces were about to wrap up hostilities, but there was an attempt on the part of many to get in their final licks. For example, I came across two trucks that were linked by a tow cable that had been wrapped once around a tree. The vehicles took turns pulling each other back and forth. In the process, the bark of the tree was ringed and its death insured. The tree had been the pride and joy of the villagers and now it was destroyed. Our intervention was limited to a couple of low passes over the scene. Unfortunately, the damage had been done.

By the time I returned to Edmonton, the position I had been assigned after Staff College had been filled by another. To my delight, I was returned to Regimental duty. We were on the eve of Canada's Centennial and I couldn't imagine a better place to spend such an exciting year. The Battalion was stationed in Victoria. LCol Kip Kirby was commanding.

Earlier I wrote of the impact that Wild Bill had on my career. Now I need to acknowledge the man who honed it. During my early days with the Regiment, Kip Kirby had been my Company Commander. He held that position in the rank of Captain. He was an exceptional soldier and spent long hours discussing the tactics of modern warfare. He was a man who thought things through. After every exercise and every tactical test, he would sit down and walk his junior Officers through the experience they had just had. It always seemed that, no matter how insignificant something might appear, he was able to help us see its overall impact on the operation. He did much to shape my capacity to lead and command.

I reached Victoria just in time to dig out my combat kit and head to the field. In my 15th year in the Army, while we were on exercise, word came through of my promotion to Major. I was busy in my Company Command Post preparing for the next phase of the exercise, when Major Dick Graham stuck his head through the flap of the tent. He extended his congratulations and put a set of crowns on my shoulders. He had found them tucked away in his things and, muttering something about not having me going around improperly dressed, headed out. As I remember Dick, he was a good-spirited guy.

Another challenge those days was a cross-island training trek. The scenario was that an enemy force had gained control of the town of Cowichan Lake and we had to dislodge them. We boarded a Destroyer to travel a few hours up the west coast of Vancouver Island. For most it was their first experience on a war ship and consequently a rewarding adventure. I suspect that, for some, there were a few moments of bonding as soldiers and sailors got to appreciate the lives the others lived.

From there we proceeded on foot along several converging routes, with a view to putting in a Battalion attack on the enemy. It was about forty miles as the crow flies, but the mountains, valleys littered with dead fall, cold streams and abandoned logging roads made the actual distance much greater. The real danger was the risky, uncertain footing.

In training a soldier for war, you confront him with every tough situation you can, so that in operations the only fear he has to overcome is that of the enemy. That's why you push him out of airplanes, down mountain sides, across raging mountain streams and through rain forests. You drive him around the clock and work him until he nearly drops. It's the only way he can learn just what he's really capable of. It's the stuff that makes winning possible when the crunch comes!

One of the many goals of this exercise was testing the Army's newly-designed combat boot. We really put it through its paces and then sent it back to the drawing board. The boot didn't breathe properly and that caused some major foot problems. You can't have that in a war. It was feedback some people didn't want to hear, but it was a very valid evaluation.

That summer each Company was put through its operational paces. My guys came through with flying colours! LCol Kip Kirby could take great satisfaction in knowing that he'd trained me well. And with that he was gone and LCol Herb Pitts was on the scene. My last close encounter with him had been on the basketball courts in Germany! Being on the Brigade staff in those years, he had played for the Headquarter's team. He knew what it took to compete.

Chapter 20
CENTENNIAL

As Canada's Centennial approached, a fellow Officer shared that he had told the Old Man that he wasn't keen on getting caught up in any of the nonsense associated with the Centennial. Actually his remark probably made it easier for the Colonel, because the guy wasn't really one that rubbed shoulders with the public too readily. Yet under normal circumstances, the boss would want to give him a share of the fun. That's the word to use: FUN.

When the opportunity presented itself, I let Colonel Herb know that anything he wanted to throw my way I would be absolutely delighted to take on. I really wanted to be involved. Boy did he take me at my word!

That year I was named as Aide to the Lieutenant Governor of the Province of British Columbia, His Honour General George C. Pearkes. I'd had a brief glimpse of him as a politician and had been unimpressed, but in this role he was truly magnificent. He and his dear lady were wonderful representatives of Her Majesty -- really wonderful.

As his Aide, the responsibilities paralleled those which I filled while aiding Princess Alexandra. In addition, my wife and I (she was very much an essential part of things) were encouraged to mix with the guests at formal functions, stimulate conversation, introduce guests who might not be familiar with one another and generally be a positive presence.

They treated Irene and me so graciously, you'd almost think they worked for us instead of the other way around. I remember Mrs. Pearkes giving Irene a package of leftovers for our girls. The functions that they hosted were lavish, so these were "out of this world" to our children. They were definitely a quantum leap forward from the leftover field rations I would bring back after a training exercise! Looking back, however,

I have to say that the kids devoured both offerings with about the same measure of enthusiasm. Aren't children great?

The Canadian Forces put on a fabulous Military Tattoo. For the uneducated in these matters, a military tattoo is a presentation of the fighting forces at their most colorful best. There usually are marching bands, athletic presentations, musical concerts and from time to time, such spectaculars as the *Feu de Joie* (Fire of Joy), to stir the nationalistic juices.

It was so good that the Americans requested it tour the USA for six months after it completed its obligations in Canada. Of note is that some of our major Canadian cities showed no interest in the presentation. I guess that's par for the course for so much of what is home grown. Ask any entertainer!

It was my privilege to command the modern scene of this military show. Captain Ron Barker, who had taken on the task of training the guys, partnered with me in this undertaking. The plot was that there were foreign agents bent on stealing a vital national secret that was at the core of an amazing, recoverable satellite. The ringleader was Stella Stiletto.

The act began as the device landed in the middle of the stadium. It was actually lowered by a cable so slim that it was almost invisible. Stella, seeing that the satellite appeared to be unprotected, pounced on it and feverishly began to take it apart to steal the secret component.

At this juncture my force went into action. We were all hidden on the roof of the stadium. On a signal, we cut loose with a half dozen 30-caliber machine guns, firing blanks of course. Then in the next 30 seconds or so, I put 100 men on the stadium field. Some of us repelled into reserved spots in the midst of the audience, while others grasped toggles thrown over "death slide" ropes and rode them from the stadium roof right onto the field. It was spectacular to watch, given that the ropes would smoke because of the friction.

Stella would, of course, take off and run like mad into the audience where she was always caught, thrown over the shoulder of the big fellow who went after her, and carried kicking and screaming back to the field of action. Then, with Stella and the satellite securely in hand, we did a tactical withdrawal from the stadium floor. We expended more ammunition in five minutes than most Units used in an entire year of field training! Boy, did we have fun and the audience loved it!

Interestingly, it was on the roof of Empire Stadium in Vancouver, as I lay watching the rehearsals of some of the other acts below, that I listened to the unfolding drama of Israel's Six Day War. What a victory it was for that tiny nation! The whole Arab world was amassed against her and she beat the pants off them!

But we weren't finished yet. "Boom, how would you like to take a mini-tattoo on the road and, starting at Hope, run it north to Prince George and out to Prince Rupert? There are about a dozen towns along that route and I would expect that they would all be delighted to have something special this year. You'd have a couple of weeks, putting on a show each night. You'll have to get on the road pretty quickly for a reconnaissance. The towns will have to take the program on the night of your choosing, because there won't be any time to backtrack. What do you say?"

As usual Colonel Herb had done his homework. The guidelines he laid down were sound. The proposal was absolutely exciting! I could hardly wait to get going!

Hope, B.C. was our first stop. What a wonderfully apt word for the experience that began to unfold ("Hope" as in "I hope we are going to make it"). You can't believe the problems in the first days of this venture! Anything that could go wrong went wrong. Vehicles broke down, show components didn't arrive, the weather was uncooperative, promises weren't met... My head didn't hit the pillow in the first 48 hours. However, there is a spirit in small towns that sets them apart. Co-operation is the byword. Very simply, we were the biggest thing to come by all year and we were excitement. The people had come to have a good time and were determined not to miss out.

After the show at the second stop, a mobile repair team arrived to change an engine in one of the trucks that we had towed along with us. There, right on the main street, the guys did the job. We had as many folks watching that operation as had turned out for the tattoo. They simply left the local fair grounds or what have you, and gathered around the break-down and its team. It was as if this was just the next attraction. They hung around for hours. When the Crew Chief finally jumped in the cab and cranked her over, a cheer went up that rivaled that at the Sky Dome years later when the Blue Jays baseball team won the World Series. They were with us all the way!

What else did we have to show them? A dismantled jeep sat on blocks in the middle of the field. From the word "Go!", a four man crew raced against the clock to put it together, jump in and drive off. It took them the better part of three minutes to do it all! Search and rescue brought in a chopper, put it through its paces to demonstrate its maneuverability, winched a casualty on board and exited up! The Navy put on its traditional cannon-crossing competition. Two teams dismantled their guns, moved them over certain obstacles (I think the idea is ship to ship), then reassembled and fired them. Repelling was demonstrated, along with the use of the "death slide". All of these men were launched from a tubular tower erected and taken down each day.

There were many displays, including one van which housed a magnificent collection of hand-painted, miniature, lead soldiers -- the handiwork of Captain Ron Barker. Each period costume had been meticulously researched to ensure a true representation. Another offered a hands-on exposure to the weaponry of an infantry battalion. In most places, the locals spiced up the grounds with food concessions, booths to sell raffle tickets for local projects and posters announcing coming events. You know the stuff of small towns.

A major component of the program was The Queen's Own Rifles band. They provided a brief concert, a marching display and a closing sunset ceremony. A local dignitary was always invited to take the salute. In one town the lady who was thus honoured stood in tears as the guys marched past. I think her name was Ma Barker. She had been the long-time Editor of the local newspaper and, for a time, mayor of the town. She was one proud Canadian!

Before I move on, I need to mention the YMCA's Centennial Year Project to promote physical fitness. They offered a very attractive collector spoon for each one hundred miles that participants could clock in the year. The conditions were that one could run no more than three miles nor less than a half mile on any given day. Over the project period it was possible to earn eleven spoons. My CSM (Company Sergeant Major) John Cresswell did just that and made sure I got started on the same path by having us launch together on January first.

Now it had been determined that, as we neared the end of the first fitness segment, we would have the Base's PR-type on hand to get a picture of us crossing the finish line together.

On the morning of February third, I got up earlier than usual and ran my miles, showered and returned to the track just as John was about to run his. He greeted me warmly and asked if I was ready to go. I explained that I had already finished, but I would hang around until he was done and then we could stage crossing the line together for the picture. I said something about having to look my best for my fans.

As John came down the home stretch, sweaty and appropriately disheveled, I pulled alongside. The picture was taken and duly published. I must say I looked fit!

John didn't forget that little incident. We both lived long enough for him to get even. A couple of years later, when I returned as CO, he took great pleasure in beating me during our annual physical fitness test. At 39 years of age, I turned in my best result ever: 1 hour and18 minutes for ten miles, but he was at least a couple of minutes ahead! No doubt he very much enjoyed the win.

For me the one disappointment of the year was that I was not awarded a Centennial Medal. The CO really tried hard to get me added to the list, but to no avail. My consolation was that I had had all of the fun. It probably didn't hurt my career either. If I remember correctly, the Colonel was very generous to me when completing my annual confidential. The relationship that he and I built continues even to this day. It will resurface a little later in this account.

Know what happened next?

You guessed it. We moved again! The Marsaws were off to Europe once more, all six of us.

Chapter 21
WATCH OUT FOR THOSE EVANGELICALS

I have often said that God determines my postings -- the Army just gets to sign off on them. After the most unusual and rewarding year of my career, Canada's 100th birthday, we were on the move again. My family and I were heading back to Germany. My new posting was that of GSO2 (General Staff Officer) of the First British Corps. For an Officer of my rank, it was the *piece de resistance* in career opportunities and God had seen fit to give it to me.

You see, in order to provide the Canadian Army the opportunity to develop its Officers for high-level staff appointments, the British War Department offered Canada one vacancy at the Headquarters of each of its major formations assigned to NATO. Mine was the gem! The Corps was commanded by "Tubby" Butler, a three-star General who, as a Brigadier, had led the British forces back in the days of the Suez crisis. He was a very personable leader and we hit it off really well.

Under him my team got to write the lion's share of the 1968 European Defense Plan for the Corps. In the routine of things, my job was to run the Operations Center at the Headquarters. It was an around-the-clock venture, with the threat of nuclear attack necessitating its complete move every 24 hours. To help you understand what that entailed, look in on "set up day" the next time a circus comes to town. Actually, even then you would only begin to get the idea, because big tents in open fields wouldn't do. Every one of our vehicles had to be hidden. That demanded a wide displacement and an extensive internal communications network. It was something else!

I was also responsible for contributing to the frequent operational briefings that the Commander demanded. It was impossible for him to be in on everything that was happening, so it was the obligation of the Operations staff to vet the mountain of information that came in and make him aware of the essentials. My boss, Colonel John Kenyon, met with me before each session to check details and then initiate the briefings. By the time I got around to giving my contribution, I usually found that he had stolen my thunder and what I had left to say wasn't all that significant. Once I got past being the new kid on the block, I decided to do something about that.

In the next briefing I opened my part with, "General Butler, Colonel John has regularly outflanked me, but today, I must confess, I've held back one goodie for my presentation." Then I proceeded to explain it. When I was finished, the good General gave me a new nickname, "Scoop Marsaw".

Another of my responsibilities was to oversee the list of indi- viduals who had a really high level of access to confidential information dealing with British and American nuclear data. On posting out of the Corps, individuals were signed off. One minute they could see certain documents, the next minute not so. The information they had accrued during their time of access was, of course, not to be disclosed.

We were in a playful mood one day when we learned that a certain person was coming in for signing off. In the "war room" of our Headquarters, there was a one-way glass window. We asked him to be seated where he could hear but not see what was going on. Behind the glass we had set up a punching bag. One of my guys would pound it with all his might and then ask the seeming recipient of the blow a classified question. "What are the yields of the shells of field weapons?" No answer. Another blow. A groan. Another question...

After several minutes of this, we commended the one behind the glass for standing up so well under interrogation. Then we called for the next guy to come in.

As our "victim" stood to enter, he got a momentary glimpse of a bloodied individual being helped on his way. The medical guys had done a super make-up job! He really looked like we had almost done him in. I'm not sure how far along it was in the whole affair before the object of our jest caught on, but from his facial expression, it looked like it took him a while.

Now, we've seen the military purpose in sending me to Germany, but what did God want? While stationed in Pakistan years earlier, I had met Gerhard and Christa Hahn, a CEF (Child Evangelism Fellowship) missionary couple from Germany. When I learned of my posting to their homeland, I wrote them immediately to tell them of my good fortune. Can you imagine my surprise to find a letter from Gerhard awaiting my arrival? They were home on furlough and living only a few kilometers from Bielefeld, the location of the Corps Headquarters. He said that I'd never be able to find him, but if I called when I reached Germany, he would come to me.

You know, if an infantry soldier couldn't find his way around, it would be a sad state of affairs. So, it being a Saturday and the day set aside for settling in, I borrowed a car and went looking. The bottom line was that that afternoon we had a delightful time of fellowship with the Hahns and a wonderful meal with the entire family. During the afternoon I learned the name of an English-speaking Pastor who lived in Bielefeld. My host urged me to look him up some time. Good idea!

On the way back to base, we did just that. In fact in only a matter of minutes we were knocking at his door. Now hold on to your hat. Would you believe that that very week he'd received a letter from an American lady whom he had met in the US, while on a course of some sort? She was arriving in Bielefeld in a few days and asked if he might meet her at the airport. The Pastor asked Irene and I to do that, because this gal would no doubt be looking for Christian fellowship and he felt we could best meet her need. We agreed.

In response to our inquiry about other English-speaking Christians he knew, we got the name and address of an Army Scripture Reader, a James Kirk (not the Commander of the

Enterprise) involved in an outreach ministry to British soldiers. He worked a bit like our Navigators who go onto campuses with the Gospel. It turned out that his home was just three doors away from the gasthof where we resided.

The significance of this fascinating chain of contacts will become evident shortly. Among other things, you will conclude that God is the Master of circumstance. He really is in charge.

"Thanks for the great day Lord. We can hardly wait to see what tomorrow holds, especially what ministry you would have us do in the next couple of years." Three options became evident. One, join the lay team who ministered in the "Free Church" (one that is not Roman Catholic or Church of England), that meets just down the road. Two, coordinate the Officers' Christian Union for the area. Three, do something for the young people, perhaps work with the Sunday School.

Within a week or two of our arrival, I visited the Anglican Sunday School. Slipping quietly into the room, I found a young soldier teaching a dozen or so kids from ages 4 to about 12. I'll never forget that experience. The subject, if you can believe it, was "the pros and cons of excommunication." He had the kids sing that great old chorus *Fight the Good Fight*.

After the youngsters were gone, I learned that the soldier had popped in a month or so back to see if he could help. The next week he was called by the guy in charge, explaining that he was quite unwell and asking him to pinch hit the next Sunday. That was the last he had seen or heard from him! Since then, he had been doing his best to carry on.

With the young soldier's agreement, I approached the boss chaplain and offered my services. I received a polite but not too enthusiastic response. He agreed to put the idea before the Church Council which, as much to his surprise as mine, quickly endorsed the proposal. I had a green light! But now what do I do?

As an Officer, the planning, deployment and management should be a snap. First, we needed some decent kids' Sunday School material. We ordered 100 sets of Gospel Light material from England. While awaiting its arrival, we set about solving the problems of a meeting place, advertising and transportation.

We were given a huge gym for our use. The problem was that it doubled as a dance hall and the smell of stale beer greeted us each Sunday. I requisitioned buses. No problem! From the very beginning the buses traveled through the various "married patches" (the servicemen's family residences) and picked up the kids. And did we have kids! Everybody wanted to go to the Canadian's Sunday School. Within a couple of weeks we had nearly 200 youngsters!

"Oh, but aren't you forgetting something? What about teachers?" Remember all those people we met in the early hours of our arrival? Not everyone ended up on my team, but those who didn't contributed other contacts, so that overnight I had a great cadre. Sure, some of the classes had 25 kids or so, but God gave me a gifted bunch of teachers. They handled the children very well!

Let me tell you about two of them. Remember the American lady? She was Barbara Chenault Duff, granddaughter of the founder and Commander of the renowned "Flying Tigers" of WW2. She was a phenomenally gifted Christian. She'd come to Germany to be the prima donna of the Bielefeld Opera. Back home she had hosted children's TV programs and was the principal vocalist for Toronto's Peoples' Church "Living Christmas Tree" for several years in the 1980s.

Then there was the spy! The Anglican chaplain was very uneasy about me and persuaded a young lady of his parish to join my teaching cadre. He apologized for imposing, but explained that there was a need to "keep an eye on those evangelicals...you've got to watch out for them, you know!"

We began teacher-training sessions and fellowship in our home. The spy came and listened. At first she was an evolutionist. She did not believe in the parting of the Red Sea. She did not believe in Noah's Ark or Jonah and his whale. She didn't believe in the necessity of being born again -- at first. She chose to change that one day, in our kitchen!

Shortly after that day, she ran into the Padre who inquired as to how she was surviving and asked if we had been caught up in any nonsense. He went on at length about our questionable interpretation of Scriptures. She listened carefully.

When he finally finished she said, "Yes, Padre, they are different -- and now, so am I. I'm one of them."

The highlight of our year was the Christmas program. The kids did a fantastic job, as did the supporting cast of chickens and a pony. The Padre was invited to conclude the day. All he said was that the audience had just witnessed "Christmas according to the Sunday School."

We had arrived in Germany with all four of our kids. For an Officer to have his entire family with him was an uncommon experience. The British way was to ship them off to boarding school. We had never even considered that possibility. Just as soon as she could, Irene marched them down for enrolment in the local British school. She was surprised to learn that they would even take young Beverley into a class for 4 and 5 year olds. This gave rise to a very humourous incident.

The next day as Irene saw the kids to school, Beverley's teacher, Miss Watkins, drew Irene aside to tell her what happened in class.

Apparently Beverley had asked, "Miss What-kins. May I borrow an eraser?"

She replied, "Certainly, Beverley dear, but we call it a rubber."

Beverley, pointing to her snowboots on the floor, said "Those are rubbers, Miss What-kins."

"No dear, those are gums."

"This is gum." said Beverley, pulling a great wad of gum from her mouth!

Every moment we could find we spent sightseeing. It was great fun walking down the street with my family, often with two girls on each arm. They were usually all decked out in the same dresses. Irene did a great job keeping them looking good, on a pretty limited budget. With four kids we didn't have much to spare, but the girls were always looking to add to their number. On one of those strolls they had a vote. It was five to one for another baby, with mother casting the dissenting ballot. By the time we were heading back to Canada, Irene was indeed expecting another child.

Heading back you say? But you just got there! That's how the British felt too, but since the command of a regiment was the issue, they took their lumps and let me go. It was March, 1969, not three years since my promotion to Major. Now it was to the rank of Lieutenant Colonel. I could hardly believe it!

One last word about Germany. Two days before our departure I was not yet satisfied with the arrangements for the Sunday School. I was concerned that the Sergeant, who was taking over my role, did not have the clout to make things happen.

At the very last minute, my doorbell rang. A Naval Officer had arrived on the scene. He had just been posted in. Why, I don't know. I greeted him enthusiastically and soon learned that he was a member of the Officers' Christian Union. I quickly came to the point of ministry. "We have a Sunday School that needs leadership. Do you have any experience with kids?"

He smiled one of the broadest smiles I've ever seen. Then he shared that the Lord has been burdening him of late about children and now he knew why. Incidentally, as a Naval Officer he was different enough to have good leverage. I guessed that the military would be just as inclined to support a sailor as they had a Canadian soldier.

But how are all the details of such a transfer back, especially with a family, worked out? Here's how it unfolded. Ernie Wesson called me in Germany soon after being appointed to take on my role at Corps. It was quite rewarding to see that, as soldiers, we had such a sense of brotherhood we could swap our things sight unseen. The Wessons would get our Opel, fridge, transformers and the likes; we'd get their Pontiac.

The last week of our tour in Germany was hectic. My replacement arrived with his family of four. The day he reached Bielefeld, his wife came down with something and was hospitalized, so Irene ended up with their children. Then, a couple of doors down, a British family experienced the tragic loss of a husband and father. Two more kids. Ten in all. Add packing and farewell parties. Every day was go, go, go. At the time we didn't appreciate how stressful this whole business was on Irene.

We made the long trek back to Canada. Reaching Trenton, we picked up the car Ernie had left for us. We drove to Ottawa for a quick briefing before heading west. The Officer who handled infantry promotions was from the Royal 22nd Regiment. His first remark was, "When I saw your name on the list, Boom, I knew you were the man! I didn't have to look any further."

It had happened that, during the practical phase of the Captain to Major promotion exams, he had been one of my assessing Officers. The Commandant of the Infantry School decided to sit in on my solution to that day's tactical problem. It was a well known fact that the Commandant's presence at a testing session meant that the candidate was in big trouble or very good. In either case, he was there to verify things for himself.

I was sailing along very nicely until the big boss decided to interject some questions of his own. I answered to the best of my ability and experience. A few minutes later he stormed off after flinging my map board over the fence and muttering something to the effect that "He's not as good as he thinks!"

After the Commandant left, my examiner breathed a sigh of relief and commended me on how well I had handled the situation. Apologizing, he asked me to start over from the beginning. He'd been so nervous with his boss there, that he hadn't taken any notes and needed them to support his assessment. That encounter, along with a pretty good track record and confidentials to back it up, opened the door to command for me. Of course I also believed that it was in the will of the Lord.

Two others met with me during that time in Ottawa. One, a senior Officer, urged me to leave religion out of my career. The other, a Padre, felt that I should turn down the promotion because it would ruin me. He was concerned that a Christian might have to make too many compromises. Free advice -- so often worth what you paid for it, but sometimes life saving!

A few days later we began the drive west to Victoria, traveling through the USA. We reached Lincoln, Nebraska in the late afternoon. The first place we stopped for lodging told us that the town was caught up in basketball fever and every nook and cranny was booked. "Sir, you won't find a thing within a hundred miles in any direction."

Irene was very tired but we had no choice but to push on. It was a good two hours before we found a town of any substance. It was very late, but there was a light on in a motel and they had room.

In the middle of the night, Irene sensed that she was in trouble. I tore over to the office to get help and found that the owner was up due to a migraine. Had she not been up, getting help would have been much more difficult. I told her that my wife thought she was losing her baby. Without hesitating, she called her personal doctor.

At that point she became very flustered, so I took over the phone. I explained that my wife was a nurse, that she was not inclined to panic even in tough situations, and that she read miscarriage. The doctor said he would call an ambulance and meet me at the hospital in five minutes. Putting Bethy in charge of the family, I followed the ambulance over.

After seeing Irene safely into the hands of the medical team at the hospital, I went back to be with the kids and await the outcome.

Irene was right about the miscarriage; the child was lost. We never asked if it was a boy or girl; however, more than once it has crossed my mind that one day up in heaven, a tall, good looking young man might walk up to me and say, "Hi, dad! Glad you're here! I'm your son. I've been waiting a long time to meet you."

Of course, with our history, it might well be a beautiful daughter. We rest in the hope of 2 Samuel 12:22, "I shall go to him, but he shall not return to me."

Chapter 22

IN COMMAND

From my earliest days with the Regiment, it was my aspiration to one day achieve command. That opportunity came far sooner than I had anticipated. As you know, my posting to the First British Corps was suddenly cut short and I was whisked back home to take over the First Battalion, The Queen's Own Rifles of Canada. I was 38 years old and, at the time, the youngest Battalion Commander in the Canadian Forces. I knew that I had very big shoes to fill. The Regiment was turning out some really fine leaders. The last two Commanding Officers were nothing short of outstanding. Both went on to become Generals.

Immediately after the handover parade the RSM (Regimental Sergeant Major -- the top non-commissioned rank in a Battalion) assembled the troops in the Mess Hall so I could address them. I don't remember much of what I said, hopefully all the right things, but most significantly I addressed the issue of faith. I realized that there were some who were concerned about "the old Bible thumper" taking command. I acknowledged that fact and suggested that they might be just a little concerned there'd be a church parade every Sunday. I assured them that would not happen. They all cheered.

"Every other Sunday." I said. And they all booed.

With that, I assured them that I wasn't there to push my faith down their throats, but hoped to prove that having the likes of me in command would make an encouraging difference.

There was a very sad note during all the excitement of this new adventure. Within days of my arrival in Victoria, my father passed away.

I not only had a fine Unit, but also got some very encouraging operational roles. One was leading the Canadian Forces'

"Mountain Warfare and Arctic Operations" Battalion. The Regiment was Canada's contribution to AMFL (Allied Mobile Force - Land). In practical terms that meant the defense of Norway. You see, in WW2 little Norway had very quickly fallen victim to Hitler's Germany. AMFL was NATO's attempt at preventing it from happening again should the Russian war machine start to roll. The Alliance had committed to putting a Brigade on the ground in Norway at the first sign of a serious threat by the Warsaw Pact nations. In the meantime, practice (war games) should provide the readiness needed to bring about success.

In preparation for the Norwegian deployment, the Unit underwent an operational evaluation. It was a near disaster! The Unit was flown to Fort St. John in northern B. C. We were equipped for Arctic operations, but there was no snow. It wasn't even cold! In the winter you don't dig down, you "sangar" up. For the most part, the shovels are not round-nosed steel spades, but broad aluminum snow scoops. We could not do a temperate exercise with winter gear, but all of a sudden that was the demand. The ground was so devoid of snow that the toboggans squealed on the stones. The Skidoos found nothing relevant to our area of deployment. The Unit suddenly became the fall guy for a major staff blunder. Someone had been so short-sighted he'd failed to check weather reports. The money wasted should have resulted in a sacking! The powers that be questioned our readiness for Norway.

The bottom line? Another exercise, another evaluation! The second took place on Vancouver Island a few miles north of Victoria, on ground much more like what we would face in Norway. Need I add, at a fraction of the cost? True, the mountains we would face in Norway were more striking than the Island's, but these ones were big enough to exercise our capacities in very irregular terrain. As always, there is value in every experience of life. The key is to know what to look for. Let me share what happened. The Unit was given its orders on a Thursday. We were told to deploy any time we wished, but be ready for the visit of LGEN GA Turcot, Commander, Mobile Command (the Army), on Tuesday. In this kind of operation, you'd seldom have such lengthy periods for the construction of defenses. I wanted to see what my guys could do in a real time scenario. So while I allowed reconnaissance of the ground on Friday and Saturday, I gave the Unit the weekend off. Deployment was to begin very early Monday morning.

We got under way in good order, but shortly after we left the main highway and began moving along the logging roads, we ran into a problem. The whole column stopped. Not knowing what was going on and now recognizing that I was working against the clock, I moved forward as quickly as I could.

At the head I saw what resembled a crowd gathered about a bargain table at Zellers. When I broke through I saw what was causing all the excitement. There in the middle of the road was a great hole the size of a family car. Looking down through the hole, I could see a chasm that would have easily held a semi-trailer. At the bottom, a mountain stream had escaped its bounds and was chewing away at the earth. The crust at the edge of the crater was only a couple of feet thick.

All during the reconnaissance phase, we had run jeeps along that very piece of road and it was strong enough to hold them up. Some time on Sunday the road had collapsed. If I had chosen to deploy earlier, among the first vehicles to have passed over that piece of ground would have been a 22-ton M113 Armoured Personnel Carrier with 11 men on board. The road would have caved in under the weight and all aboard would probably have died! Thank you, Lord, for Your timing!

We moved ahead into position and worked like mad. On Tuesday, about an hour before the General arrived, we had the most beautiful snowfall I have ever seen. The individual flakes were bigger than Toonies and utterly blanketed the whole area. When I took the General forward of our positions to look at them from the enemy's perspective, he could see nothing. Our concealment was superb!

He looked around the positions and had us launch an advance to contact the enemy. After an hour or so he called a halt. He talked to my guys and sent us home. Conclusion? Handled it with flying colours! An absolutely first-class Battalion! Approved for deployment to Norway!

Canada's role was to have a Company there in 24 hours and an entire battle group in seven days. The Queen's Own were the major component of the Canadian contribution and I was in command of it all. The overall size of the force was a Brigade Group. The other two Battalions came from Britain and Italy. Germany supplied the Armour Regiment, each Battalion brought its own artillery, and the Americans added a lot of the bits and pieces that make a force of this size work.

There were about 1200 men and a flight of six Huey helicopters in my command. We had enough Skidoos to move one whole Company, M113s (Armoured Personnel Carriers) sufficient for another and snowshoes for all. The choppers could do a good job of moving a Rifle Company in two lifts and the better part of a battery of light guns in one. This entire force was airlifted to Norway by the RCAF Transport Command.

The NATO formation was directed by an Italian Brigadier. That fact brings me to one of the funniest anecdotes of my time in command. We had been engaged for the better part of a war games day, trying to secure a mountain pass from a Norwegian Unit playing the role of enemy.

Late that night the Brigadier came to my CP (Command Post) to issue new orders. He wanted me to pull my Unit back, move to the opposite flank of our force, come under command of a Norwegian Brigade (good guys this time) and support them in an attack. Mainly, this move was designed to test the mechanics of pulling off such an operation. Differing language and operating procedures would make this quite a challenge. You'd be amazed at how well many Europeans speak our language. The Italian Commander was a good case in point. He was not convinced of his mastery of English and attempted to say every detail of his orders three or four different ways, to ensure that I understood him. In fact, what he said was always clear the first time. So I began to use the colloquial expression, "I'm with you, General." meaning, "I've got it." I must have used that phrase a few dozen times while he was going on and on. I just wanted to get on with the new job he was handing out.

Well, after he left me, indeed just outside my Command Post, he turned to the Canadian Liaison Officer assigned to his Headquarters and asked, "What's with the Colonel? He keeps saying he's with me. Of course he's with me! He's sitting right there, isn't he?" Humour in uniform.

At the close of his briefing, the Commander had added that road conditions were treacherous. If I didn't think I could pull it off, I didn't really have to move. You see, he wanted nothing to do with casualties or at least he didn't want the responsibility for any. So with that use of a "notwithstanding clause," he exonerated himself of any ill that might befall us.

So what was I to do about the assignment? It was clearly time for prayer. Oh, not to ask the Lord whether or not I should go, but for His mercy during it. I had my orders and they would be carried out. Hey, we Canadians weren't a bunch of wimps! There wasn't a Commander alive that could give the Rifles a task we couldn't pull off! I knew that's how my men felt and it was confirmed moments later when my Battle Adjutant, Major John Sharp, dropped into my CP to report that he had already ordered up the transport. "How soon do you see us crossing the start line, sir?" Incidentally, John went on be a General.

In all fairness, I need to say that the Commander's assessment of the roads was valid. In one short stint, my driver lost control of the Jeep three times and each time we pinballed our way along until we came to a halt. The roads were like huge Olympic bobsled runs! The shoulders were piled high with snow and coated with ice.

Further proof of their severity was seen post-exercise. An M113, piled high with the crews' personal gear, was halted at a sharp bend in the road. The grade sloped precipitously toward the downhill side of the feature it ran along. As they were waiting to move on, the carrier began to slip sideways. Reaching the edge, which in this case had no mound of snow, it rolled over and came to rest against some trees. The whole thing happened so slowly that there were no injuries at all!

As for the move of the entire Battalion, it was accident free. In fact we accomplished the shift in nearly two hours less than the tactical planners had anticipated. That kind of messed up the enemy who had hoped to ambush my column, but we had cleared the point of contact before they got into position.

Note that on military exercises the controllers know what both sides are doing, so they take advantage of that awareness to introduce events that will present different tactical challenges. That's the essence of training.

Orders awaited me at the new location and in response I launched one of my Companies via snowshoes in a night encirclement operation. At first light the Battalion moved forward in a frontal attack and the enemy began to withdraw. They found themselves trapped by my Company that had taken up position in the rear. I was so proud of my guys!

At the conclusion of this "Arctic Express" exercise, I called a huddle of all Officers and NCOs. I commended them on their performance, but reminded them how thankful we ought to be for coming through the whole thing unscathed. Some others had not been so fortunate. The Padre closed in a prayer of thanksgiving. He guessed that one would have to go back a long way to find the last time that had happened, if there were a last time. Then the Battalion hit the hay. They were so tired!

It is important to realize that the Norwegian venture was only one experience an Infantry Battalion might face. Life in a Regiment is an unending chain of adventures. For instance, the Unit already knew it was going to Cyprus for a six-month tour of duty the following year. Preparation was already in the back of our minds. Between now and then it was train, train, train.

An interesting facet of that training occurred back home just as our summer concentration was concluding. Word had reached Provincial authorities that the U.S. Black Panthers rebel group had decided to come to Vancouver to help some local dissidents "liberate" Stanley Park. The city requested federal assistance to meet the threat. We were it, so the Battalion was deployed to Camp Chilliwack. Major Derrick Bamford, my Second-in-Command, supervised refresher training dealing with aid to the Civil Power Operations. From a soldier's point of view, it was essentially reviewing crowd control procedures, the quelling of riots and the like.

A police liaison team soon visited us. They hoped they would not have to call on us, but were glad to know we were there to back them up. As things went, the Panthers never got across the border, so the "rumble" never occurred. Talk about disappointment! You have no idea how much the men were looking forward to some real action. When it didn't occur they felt cheated. I, for one, was pleased with the outcome. It's almost impossible to undertake such things and come out smelling like a rose. There's always someone claiming foul. The bonus was that we had the best riot control training I'd experienced. There's nothing like a real threat to sharpen interest. Even the most lethargic paid close attention!

Our return to Victoria from Germany created a unique opportunity for me. 1966-1968 was the first period when I was long enough in one place to be involved in church administration.

I'd made a lot of friends at Central Baptist Church and during those years I led their Christian Service Brigade. When I arrived it included 34 men and boys; when I left for Europe there were 34 leaders! It was going great guns -- the largest operation of its kind on the west coast.

Remember that in my opening address I'd spoken to my men about church parades? Once during my tour I took them to Central, where Dr. John Moore was pastoring. Pastor John's message was entitled "The Gospel in a Nutshell." It was a great encouragement to know that almost all of my soldiers had heard the way of salvation at least once.

Central's retired missionary, Ivan Albutt, was to speak to the young people. The goal was to make them aware of the persecution of the church in many parts of the world. He asked if I had ideas on how to illustrate the repression being experienced. No problem! Jumping in with both feet, I set up a section raiding party. They entered the church in full combat gear soon after the evening program began. Bursting into the meeting room, they declared that this was an illegal assembly and ordered everyone out. One lad broke for the fire exit. As it swung open, he was greeted by a carbine-toting soldier who herded him back into the room and out of the building. Quite unnerved, the youths retired to the leader's home where, by candlelight, they discussed what they had learned.

As usual, there was a humorous side to the event. I'd issued my guys strict orders to do all they could to avoid physical contact. If any youth decided to play hero and throw a punch, they were to just take it. The leaders were in on the venture, so if things got out of hand they would call a halt. If that happened, the troops were to assemble in a neutral corner, so to speak, and leave the building as quickly as possible. I'm pleased to say that there was no problem with the young people; however, there just happened to be a meeting of the Church Executive Committee that evening. I had said to clear the building, so the Committee got ousted too!

Chapter 23
OPERATIONAL IMMEDIATE

At this point the Unit was stationed at Work Point Barracks, a military garrison on the Maritime Command Base of Esquimalt. In order to get oneself understood, it was important to have a working knowledge of the marine context. In February, 1969, we had a bad fire in the Unit's motor transport building. In an effort to speed up repairs, I sent the following wire:

OPERATIONAL IMMEDIATE 161500Z JUN 69

FM 1 QOR OF C ESQUIMALT
TO CANFORBASE ESQUIMALT
UNCLAS A 709
FOR COMD BASE ESQUIMALT. URGENT. HMCS QUEEN'S OWN RIFLES EXPERIENCED FIRE IN ITS ENGINE ROOM FEB 69. HEAT CAUSED GAPING HOLE IN BULKHEAD. SHIP STILL UNDER WAY BUT TAKING WATER BADLY, ESPECIALLY DURING NORWESTER. REPAIRS URGENTLY REQUIRED. MARSAW, SHIP'S CAPTAIN.

Base, undaunted, replied with:

IMMEDIATE 161616Z JUN 69

FR CANFORBASE ESQUIMALT
TO 1 QOR OF C ESQUIMALT
UNCLAS BCOMD 050
YOUR 161500Z UNDER ACTIVE CONSIDERATION. IT HAS BEEN DETERMINED PLUGGING GAPING HOLE IN YOUR BULKHEAD WOULD COST ABOUT $36,000. RESULTANT GAPING HOLE IN BASE COFFERS MIGHT WELL SINK THE WHOLE BLOODY FLEET. FREWER FLEET DEP. CAPT.

Actually we had a very good relationship with Base and were really well supported. Given that they held the purse strings, it tended to be pretty much one sided, but there was an occasion when we proved to be a big help. The civil servants had gone on strike and, as things go, it wasn't long before there were a lot of little maintenance needs surfacing. I'm not sure how the Base Commander knew of it, but he called and asked if I had a little group of guys that might be able to do some fixing up for him. He was, of course, speaking of our Pioneer Platoon. No problem! That morning a crew of four reported for work, undertook and completed all the tasks that they had been given, and went back for more. After a day or two everything was pretty shipshape and they returned to the Unit.

Shortly after, I got a call from the boss. "What do you feed those guys? I have never seen the likes of the enthusiasm with which they tackled things around here. If the regular crew were anything like them, we could run the base on half the staff!"

Now, the Navy had positioned its band on the Pacific coast. They were an incredible collection of professionals. My little band was made up of anti-tank gunners. Gunners first and bandsmen second, not one was a professional musician. If the truth be known, nothing could have been more incongruous. When a 106 Recoilless Rifle goes off, the gunners are probably deaf for the better part of a day. Over the years, no matter how careful one might be, there would be some hearing loss. How could they be expected to play anything on key?

It was a matter of finding something for which the training of bandsmen could be blended and, in this case, the Anti-tank Platoon fit best. To be a gunner for this Platoon, you also had to like music. To be able to play music was even better. In one of my bolder moments, I asked the base Commander to lend me a Band Sergeant for a while, say for six months. I needed help to sharpen up my musicians and he agreed. Even more than expected, the Sergeant's impact was almost miraculous.

At this point I need to jump ahead three months, because not only did this sailor join the Unit, but he went to Cyprus with us. As his time for going home approached, he asked to see me. "Sir, I know the Unit has three more months to serve here. I do remember that, when I came to Cyprus, it was agreed that it would be for just three months. But sir, I can't go home now. It would almost be like deserting. Could you get permission for me to stay on? My wife said it's okay if the Admiral agrees." Bless his heart! He's probably the only sailor walking around with the Cyprus Service Medal. What does that say about the spirit of an Infantry Battalion? At its best, it is downright contagious!

Shift gears again -- back to Canada. Anyone who has seen *Bridge Over the River Kwia* surely has thought it would be great fun to blow one up -- at least the males have. I wanted to do just that, so I went looking. Off the main roads, British Columbia is a maze of logging trails with some pretty substantial trestle bridges capable of supporting fully-loaded logging trucks. It wasn't too hard to find an abandoned one. The good news was that it was practically side by side with the one they built to replace it. What a wonderful training scenario!

There's a military operation known as the "close bridge garrison". It almost always occurs in the setting of a troop withdrawal. This garrison is assigned the defense of the key bridge across which the withdrawing forces must pass, after which they blow it up. Obviously, this bridge is deemed to be so important that it must not fall into enemy hands. Sometimes tactical situations happen such that the bridge has to be destroyed before all the friendly forces can get across. It's a tense and dynamic operation of war.

Having found the two bridges, we worked out a comprehensive plan to defend the new one and, as the battle unfolded, to withdraw across that bridge and blow up the old one. "How do you rig a bridge for destruction?" you ask. Basically you must position the explosives at each key supporting base and connect each explosive by wires to the central point where the explosion is to be triggered. The work is often undertaken in some very precarious positions, such as just above raging rivers, thus making it quite a dangerous undertaking. As can be seen on our front cover, there are a lot of supporting timbers in a wooden trestle! To add realism, I ordered the Pioneer Platoon to set the charges under cover of darkness.

At first light, the final elements that had been deployed forward of the bridge fought their way back and across. Then I called a pause in the action, so everyone could have a daylight look at the effort that went into preparing a bridge for destruction.

That being done, we blew her up! The whole thing was observed from high ground sufficiently far back to be out of reach of any flying debris. The destruction of key supports led to the targeted section collapsing like a deck of cards, with falling timbers pulling others down with them. In just moments, it was over. That bridge was about six stories high, so it made a great splash! Whoopee!

It was on an exercise of a similar nature that I had a glimpse of the kind of stuff that heroes are made of. This time we were attacking and reached a bridge that was heavily defended. It spanned a deep, fast flowing mountain stream. There was just no way to take it frontally. I needed to get troops in behind the defenders. I tasked one of my young Officers with finding a crossing place upstream from the bridge.

Two hours later he returned to report that it was impossible. Of course I wasn't willing to accept that so, turning to a Sergeant with whom I had served for many years, I simply but forcefully said, "Get me a crossing." Actually, to this point I had not seen the condition of the stream myself; however, I knew that in the mountains changes can occur quite quickly. Flash flooding is frequent and adds a very dangerous component to any mission.

Considerable time passed before the message got back that he was across and a rope bridge was under construction. I had already put two Companies (about 270 men) on standby. At that point, I shortened their notice to move to 30 minutes. Then I went forward to see the progress the Pioneers were making building the bridge. The stream was a ragging torrent! I commended the Sergeant on what he had accomplished and asked him how in the world he had done it. His answer was a simple statement of facts. "Well sir, I just tied a long rope around me, anchored one end to a tree and ordered ten guys to haul me out if I got in trouble. Then I jumped. It took four tries. The biggest problem was that the water was damn cold!"

That night nearly two hundred men crossed that little bridge. At the midpoint, each was up to his waist in icy water. That took courage and the more so because, not a month before, one of our men had drowned in just such a stream while doing a rubber raft descent. Each one of those men had a character building experience that night. It was the kind of stuff they talked about for years.

"Remember when the Old Man put us across that bloody mountain stream? Boy, that was scary! Did you hear how the Sarg first got over...?"

Now that I've mentioned it, perhaps this would be a good place to go back in time and tell you how we lost Rifleman George. Troops were deployed in four small rubber rafts coming downstream that day, to train in handling rubber boats and increase their awareness of waterways in mountain terrain. He was in the third boat. Just before a waterfall, the stream widened. There, the crews had to go ashore and carry their boats around the falls before continuing their descent.

George made it to the bank of the stream. He had one foot on the shore and one in the raft. Realizing that he hadn't taken his weapon, he reached for it and while slinging it, slipped, hit his head on some rocks and apparently knocked himself out.

In an instant he was beyond reach and over the falls. A downstream search failed to locate his body. We began to believe that it was trapped in one of the whirlpools below the falls. As I mentioned, the stream was wide at this point. What I didn't say is that there were two falls, like at Niagara Falls.

I tasked the men to build a diversion so the bulk of the water would pass over the eastern falls. (George had disappeared over the other.) Working waist-deep in a frigid mountain stream, they filled and positioned sandbags to divert the water from the western branch. Of course we certainly didn't want to lose another soldier, so care in ensuring one's footing was absolutely vital. They did it! Then they went after the body of their buddy and got him. It is absolutely amazing what a battalion can do when it comes to the crunch. Commanding one was a privilege and a pleasure, but losing one of my men was not. It was the sobering reality of the price of war and I often reflected on what I might have done to prevent the loss.

Somewhere in the mix of things I gave my guys training in living off the land. In war operations you have enormous liberty. You can scrounge, trap, trade or scavenge food; however, that just won't do in peace time. Steal a pig from a local farmer and you'll get your backside full of buckshot!

So what I did was order some live chickens, one for every two men. When they came through the food line, each pair got a raw potato and a live chicken to share with one another. You have never seen the likes of what ensued! The country boys had their bird's head off, the creature gutted and cooking in nothing flat. The city lads were something else. Some birds got away and the guys went tearing through the woods in hot pursuit. Some just couldn't bring themselves to kill the creatures, preferring instead to make them section mascots.

Invention is said to be the mother of necessity. I think that if they'd been just a little hungrier, my idea might have worked a whole lot better!

Chapter 24

THE END OF AN ERA

On April 26,1970, we celebrated our Regiment's110th birthday and the next day paraded as the Third Battalion of the Princess Patricia's Canadian Light Infantry (PPCLI): the Princess Pats. The cartoon on the editorial page pictured the Officers' Mess bar with a collection of distraught members. It was captioned, "Cut to ribbons...Wiped out...Totally annihilated...By our own side." The only consolation was that we were exchanging membership in the most decorated Regiment in Canadian history for membership in another excellent, wonderfully-storied Unit.

The change came about in large part because the Liberal Government of the time was bent on saving money. They decided to remove three Regiments from the regular order of battle. Besides the Queen's Own, the Black Watch and the Canadian Guards also bit the dust. I have to say that we are still paying the price for that decision. Our army really is short of manpower. As a consequence, some soldiers face repeated deployments to war-ravaged arenas such as Afghanistan.

The occasion was marked by a phenomenal assembly of Riflemen. Across the nation, the Queen's Own pulled out all the stops to be part of this historic moment. Offers of assistance came in from all corners. One that I took up was that of Major Ron Werry. Most knew him best by his nickname, "Awful." He had earned it because of his capacity to tell some of the most fantastic tales with such conviction, that there were few in his acquaintance who had not fallen victim. He expressed a willingness to coordinate the meeting of all the VIPs. With him in that role, one could guarantee that the guests would arrive in good spirits.

Good old Bill Mountain, the Regimental Adjutant, reminded me of the peril, but I bought in anyway.

Ron personally met many, including his fellow Winnipegger, Colonel Big Dan Osborne. Loading the Colonel's kit in the back of the staff car, Ron casually mentioned that it was too bad Dan hadn't arrived in dress uniform.

As they pulled away from Victoria's Pat Bay Airport, Dan asked why the uniform. "Well, you know what Colonel Boom is like. I think he has a Quarter Guard at the main entrance to the camp, prepared to fall out on the arrival of each special guest. You'll have to inspect the guys and it would have been great if you'd been dressed for the occasion. A picture of you doing that might have been a nice momento. But no matter, you'll look great regardless of how you're dressed...still, it would've been nice."

"Of course all that stuff is in my bags. If I had only known..."

"Don't worry about it, sir. Nothing can be done now. We certainly don't have time to stop. I promised to get you to Work Point just as quickly as possible. The Regimental fathers have some business they want to discuss and would like you to be in on it."

"Look, Ron. If you ride up front with the driver, I could probably change in the back seat as we are moving along. Let's get my kit. I'd hate to disappoint the fellows."

Now visualize a six foot something, 240 pound Colonel changing in the back seat of a car cruising down a busy highway. One moment it was speed up; the next, slow down. The goal was to ensure that nobody was so situated in an adjacent vehicle that he or she could look in on the unfolding drama. After all, the Colonel had to be protected against a charge of indecent exposure or the likes!

Eventually the task was completed. The Colonel, now arrayed in his regimental best, sat anticipating the moment of his arrival.

The car approached the main entrance, the barrier went up, the Commissionaire saluted smartly and they passed straight through. No one came storming out of the guard house. Indeed the Duty Sergeant didn't even look up from his desk where he was visible through the window.

"Gee, sir...I was sure there was supposed to be a Quarter Guard. I'm so sorry that you went to all that trouble!"

"Werry!" stormed the Colonel, "Up to your old tricks again! When are you going to learn...No, when am I going to learn?"

But I doubt that Ron will ever change. And really, we wouldn't want him to, would we?

Ron had arrived a couple of days early for the gala and had almost immediately headed for my quarters to see my family. The children recognized him as he walked towards the house and ran to see him. Now it just so happened that the sole on Ginny's shoe had torn half off during play, so it flapped as she ran. Seeing this, Ron reached into his wallet, pulled out a ten dollar bill and expressed something to the effect, "You poor kid! Things must be really tough. Take this and get yourself some new shoes."

She ran straight to her mom, waving the ten spot and shouting, "Look what Uncle Ron gave me!"

That evening at a small gathering for those who had arrived early, Irene wore her oldest heels, a pair with a small hole in the sole. For some time, she sat opposite Ron, with her legs crossed, waggling her old shoe more or less at him. She had said to me earlier, "If he gives me ten bucks, he won't get it back." But alas, he never took the bait. How do you beat the master at his own game?

The *Feu de Joie* was the focal point of the final ceremonial parade. Let me explain. History reveals that at the end of a victorious campaign, soldiers often celebrated by firing their rifles into the air. This parade square rendition brings discipline to the event and provides observers with a spectacular experience. In this ceremony, soldiers are brought to the "Present" position. They stand in double file with a loaded weapon held at shoulder level, pointed to the sky.

On the command "Commence!" the first man in line pulls his trigger. Each successive soldier does likewise, taking his cue from the report of the weapon immediately ahead of him in the line. In that manner a couple of hundred rifles will, in sequence, be fired in two or three seconds. It sounds like rapid-fire machine guns, but it's the product of a regiment of disciplined soldiers.

So often one looks back on an event and wishes that something might have been done just a little differently. Given the opportunity to do it over, I would now halt the Battalion short of the reviewing stand and invite all the Riflemen watching from the sidelines to join in the final march past.

That would have almost emptied the stands. Indeed only the wives, kids and a handful of friends would have been left, but it would have added just one more glorious dimension to what was an entirely fitting finale. At this point, I'll just have to pass the idea on to a future leader.

Colonel JGK Strathy, Colonel of the Regiment, took the salute.

Chapter 25
CYPRUS

Next stop: Cyprus! In preparation while still in Canada, I did a number of things. For example, the Battalion purchased two dozen tape recorders. The idea was to take twelve with us and leave twelve at home. Families would borrow one for a week at a time and listen to a tape sent from hubby/dad or send him a message. But more about that later.

As our time to go to Cyprus drew ever closer, the pace of preparation accelerated. One of the early signs to the community that something was stirring was the construction of a Cyprus-like observation bunker on the lawn just forward of our main entrance. It was manned night and day with a UN blue helmeted soldier, armed with a semi-automatic weapon.

Weeks before the Battalion deployed, I visited Cyprus for a reconnaissance and operation briefing. The Canadian role with the UN mission was the maintenance of peace in Nicosia, the nation's capital. There the opposing Turkish and Greek forces sat on either side of the "green line", a demarcation that in some places was no wider than a village lane! While on orientation, I met VIPs on the Turkish and Greek sides, as well as key personalities with whom I'd be working. Among the last of my visits was to the American Communications Station. I was ushered into the Commander's office to meet Colonel Giocano, an Italian American.

"Colonel," I said, "You have no idea how disappointed I am. All day I've been meeting Cypriots on both sides and coming away without the slightest idea of how to pronounce their names. I felt sure that when I got here I'd run into a Brown, Jones or Smith." He apologized and leaned forward to push a button on his intercom. "Exec, will you come in for a moment?" (a pause) "Colonel Marsaw, meet Major Green." That led to a discussion about names, during which I related the fact that Colonel Thorold, my very indirect namesake, played a major role in the battle of 1812, a war in which Canadians more than held their own against the Americans, even capturing Detroit. "We really won, you know." Giocano turned out to be a bit of an historian and in the end I invited him and his Officer to a Mess dinner. He agreed to give us a talk on the 1812 conflict. I promise I'll come back to that.

Then, just like that, we were there. Compared to our deployment to Norway, going to Cyprus was a cup of tea. We could have handled it with one arm behind our back, so to speak.

While there, one goal was to learn of any English-speaking Christian presence on the Island. Eureka, I found a little community church and a Scottish Pastor. The bad news was that he was retiring and leaving for home the week before our Unit's arrival. Remember what I said earlier about God determining my postings and the army just being given the right to sign off on them? During my six months on Cyprus, I preached in that little church at least once a month. The new Pastor, whom I never met, flew in the week after the Battalion left for home. "Master of circumstance" He is. Fascinating, isn't it?

To say that Cyprus was a graveyard would be too strong, but it had spelled the doom of many a marriage. Because of the political unrest between the Greeks and the Turks, its tourist industry was drastically depressed. If you had an adventurous spirit you could go there and have a great holiday for next to nothing. British secretaries knew that and it became one of their favorite haunts. In fact, during the summer the place was swarming with them. Add to that mix substantial UN forces, many of them single and all a long way from home, and you've got a potentially explosive situation! My goal was to keep the peace on the Island -- and at home. Good communication seemed to be key to success.

My Headquarters was downtown, just outside the walls of the old city and within yards of its swankiest hotel, The Lydra Palace. The rooms on one side of the hotel overlooked the

Turkish lines, so they were not rented out. During a period of heightened tension a few years after our tour, a young Officer went out on the balcony of one of those rooms and got shot. The Turks didn't appreciate his cavalier spirit.

My residence was in a small bungalow situated by a stream right in the middle of "no man's land." That means it was between the lines. The Turkish forces were on a commanding hillside to the north and the Greek forces in the built-up area on the ground to the south. To get home I drove out through the Greek positions, down the hill and in. There my driver, my Mercedes and I lived quite comfortably.

Right from the beginning I wanted both sides to know that the new "Muktar" was really determined to do his job. So at random times of the day and night, I drove right along the dividing line. Actually, it wasn't a surprise to anyone. You can be sure that, just as soon as the Mercedes' lights went on, the word went out on both sides that the Canadian Commander was on the move. They would be ordered to keep their eyes open and report my progress.

A couple of times during our tour I parked my vehicle right between the opposing forces who were caught up in a local dispute. I sat there reading a book while my local Commander sorted out the problem. Unrest could occur from the simplest circumstances. For example, if a field emplacement was in need of repair, you can be sure that one side would accuse the other of inching forward under the pretext of fixing something. Of a truth, they were always trying to gain an inch here and a foot there.

To cater to this kind of thing on a larger scale, each of the UN contingents had to provide a quick-response team. If serious fighting should break out and rounds were flying, the force Commander wanted the diplomats of all the countries to bring pressure to bear on the opposing forces to cease fire and not just on the nation in whose zone the problem occurred.

Getting the diplomats to move would be a lot easier if some of their soldiers were being shot at. The Commander wanted to be sure that we were in on the action. And, if my memory hasn't failed me, the other contingents were from Ireland, Sweden and Finland. The only time that the quick response team was used in our day was as a result of some unrest in the Swedish sector, way out on the Cypriot panhandle at the extreme northeast corner of the Island. My guys were so well organized, they beat the Swedes to their own designated rendezvous. But then, the Swedes were always late!

That statement leads me to a unique event. The Force Commander was Indian General Prim Chan. He thought it would be a good idea to have days set aside for each contingent to entertain and inform the others about their homeland. What a great idea! No problem! I didn't have to think twice about who I should task with the job. "Get Bob McDiarmid in here on the double! This is right up his alley." The Unit had a lot of really good young Officers with a wide variety of talents. Some time back Bob had worked with me when I headed up the United Appeal in Victoria. He had shown real imagination.

Like me, Bob had had the opportunity of visiting EXPO '67. There on screen we had witnessed some fabulous displays of Canadianna, a multimedia spectacular. "Bob, I want you to come as close as you can to duplicating that presentation. We can't expect to get our hands on the electronic wizardry that they had. It will all have to be done manually, but I'm convinced the material is out there to make it happen."

In the next couple of weeks, letters poured out of my office. We approached the Tourist Bureau of each Canadian Province and Territory, telling them what we were doing and asking for 35 mm slides. We obtained the National Film Board's *Helicopter Canada* and got a super, action-packed recruiting film: no words, just music and lots of hustle. And then we were loaned prints of the highlights of the previous year's Grey Cup and Stanley Cup finals.

Renting the largest theater in Nicosia, we began production. In the end we ran two films on the main screen at the same time, one above the other, using one sound track. To the right and left of these on the same screen, we projected the 35 mm pictures, again one above the other. The projectionists were rehearsed so as to advance their cameras as the movie commentator guided us across our fabulous Canada. Each projector had about one hundred slides.

Our big day came. We were all set to go. Everyone was there but the Swedes. Word came in that they had some problem or other, but were on the move again and expected to be twenty minutes late. We waited and we waited. Finally they arrived. With regrets, they rushed into the theater and, in the process, managed to kick over one of the projection tables, sending hundreds of slides flying every which way!

Now what? Bob said that those guys knew their slides so well that in five minutes they could put them back in order. Would you believe they did that from memory? It was a great day!

Earlier you heard of General Prim Chan. Shortly after arriving, I was a guest at his home for dinner. His wife was a delightful lady. In the conversation, they learned that I had served in their country in 1965. I made the point of emphasizing how much I enjoyed eastern foods. In fact, I shamelessly volunteered to fill any empty chair at their table, if there were any last minute cancellation of a future dinner guest! "A" for effort.

One day when the Chans were having a very high-powered dinner, I sneaked the Unit band over to their home. It was built kind of up in the air, with the ground floor open to the elements to enhance cooling. That's where I positioned the band. While they played a little concert, I sat down the street in my car, just in case I had misread things and created a problem. The good General was absolutely thrilled. Martial music always seemed to put some extra curl in his mustache and maybe even a little more kick in the curry.

When we'd worn the badge of the Queen's Own, the Officers' Mess table was graced by an 1860 Enfield Rifle. That was the year the Regiment came into existence. Now that we were the Patricias we had to exchange the weapon for a 1914 Ross, for that was the year the PPCLI was born. In a conversation at which our navy friends were present, before our Battalion left for Cyprus, I had casually made that need known. Would you believe that one of them had a connection with the Ross family in Montreal and was certain that they would help us out? He promised to get on it right away.

While we were keeping the peace in Cyprus, the rest of the Canadian Army was trying to do the same thing back home. It was the time of the FLQ crisis. Personally I was glad to be out of the country. It wasn't a very pleasant thing. The reason I even mention it is because something significant to the battalion got entangled in the unfolding national drama.

Good news! The 1914 Ross was obtained. The courier, who was hand-carrying the wrapped Ross with him to Victoria, was trying to board an Air Canada jet right in the midst of the tightest security our nation had ever experienced. Just as he was about to walk through the metal detector, he was stopped and asked what he was carrying. He replied, "A rifle."

"Sir, we don't find that very funny. Aren't you aware that it's a federal offense to even joke about such things as highjacking and weapons?"

"I'm not joking. You asked me what I have and I said it's a rifle -- and it is. It's a 1914 Ross rifle. I'm taking it to Victoria at the express request of the Third Battalion of the Princess Pats."

"1914? Will it still fire? C-C-Could you unwrap it?"..."Well, I guess it's okay, but we'd better stow it in the hold."

Another thing that happened back home while we were on peacekeeping duty was a visit by Evangelist Barry Moore to the rear party (our men who stayed behind in Canada). I had tried to get him to Cyprus, but that wasn't possible. In my absence, Major Kent Foster (later a General and in command of the Canadian Forces during the Oka crisis) was in charge of the Unit's Home Station. He was a little uneasy about this whole business, but now looks back on it as quite an experience. Barry, a gifted speaker with an amazing ability to read his audience, won my guys over with his opening story. He spoke of reaching heaven and being given a piece of chalk to go to a great blackboard in the sky and record all his sins. "As I started up the ladder, someone almost stepped on my hand. Guys. It was your CO coming back down for more chalk!" They loved it!

Not long before Christmas a near tragedy struck. One of my fellows, returning from patrol, entered the room he shared with another soldier and found him busy writing a letter. When he greeted his buddy there was no response. A moment passed and he again announced his arrival. Again, no acknowledgement. Finally he protested, "If you don't speak to me, I'll shoot you." Nothing. Then he pointed his pistol at the middle of his friend's back, pulled the trigger and it went off.

The lad was rushed to the British Military Hospital. I was only minutes behind him on the road and managed to reach his side just before he went into surgery. Holding his hand, I asked God to bring him through. I wondered afterwards how many COs had ever had the opportunity to pray with one of their soldiers at such a moment. I knew it was possible that he would die, but I left convinced that he would come through and praise the Lord, he did!

Well, no matter how unintentional the whole thing might have been, the perpetrator was guilty of a very serious offense that could not just be swept under the carpet. The decision as to what should be done was mine. Some urged court martial, pointing out that the case was potentially so complicated, I might soon find myself in over my head. Others thought that my powers were utterly inadequate, because I could only sentence a man to a maximum of 90 days. The likely charge of attempted manslaughter warranted far more than that.

I was convinced of the unintentional nature of the offense and determined that I would not give one of my soldiers over into another's hands. In short order he was on his way back to Canada to serve out his time. I asked my troops not to write home about the matter. As things worked out, at tour's end I was able to arrange for the perpetrator to board one of the aircraft at Trenton returning the Unit back to Victoria. That enabled him to deplane at Pat Bay Airport right along with the rest of us. If my sources are reliable, not a whole lot of folks knew about the accident or about his time in the slammer.

It's hard to know exactly how the matter impacted my relationship with the Battalion. I'm sure that a good number must have reflected on my initial remarks about the encouraging difference I hoped to bring to command. Trials are always of interest -- some, of course, more than others. My concern was that outcomes were not only just, but appeared to be as well.

Ah yes, I promised to tell you about the Mess dinner with the Americans. First I must acknowledge that Colonel Giocano gave a scholarly presentation on the war of 1812. I learned a lot. But at its end, I argued that the outcome seemed yet to be indecisive. Because we were representative groups of the two nations involved in the conflict, we ought to take it upon ourselves to resolve the matter that very night.

I proposed that we play a game of Blowball and that thereby, once and for all, we'd resolve this ancient dispute. That being agreed, I informed the Americans of the absolutely impartial nature of the two I had chosen to officiate: one Chinese and one Russian. They introduced themselves.

My Chinese Officer spoke first. He said his heritage gave him the capacity to deal with the most explosive issues without the least inclination to partiality. But then he expressed gratitude to the Canadian Government for its world leadership in acknowledging the sovereignty of the People's Republic of China. At the time, the USA had not yet done that.

Surprise! My Russian-speaking Officer had been coached to proceed along the same line. As it turned out, the Yanks had a Russian speaker themselves and, before I knew it, the two Ruskies were hugging each other, slapping backs and "comrading this and comrading that". We had a great night!

Remember the recorders I bought in Canada, leaving half for the families at home and bringing half to the field? On Cyprus I allowed my guys to carry recorders on patrol and encouraged them to record the events of their day as they carried out their duties. We also arranged with a local radio station to have a weekly hour-long request show. One week those in Victoria could call in requests and send greetings; the next week, they could play the tape of the program from Cyprus.

It was a popular hour and the bonus was that Victoria got to learn a whole lot more about their Battalion and its adventures. Best of all, we were able to arrange a two-week visit to the Island for every wife who wanted to come. Most grabbed the opportunity. Plus, we got ourselves on Central Church's support prayer list. That was a bonus!

As things unfolded, my postal detachment reported to me the rewarding news that barely half way through our tour we had already surpassed the previous Unit in our level of correspondence. It's so encouraging to be able to record now, over four decades after the fact, that there wasn't one marriage breakup arising out of the Battalion's Cyprus adventures.

Wednesdays always brought an air of excitement to the mission. That day the aircraft from Trenton arrived. With it came the mail, the bits and pieces to keep the operation moving smoothly, guys being posted in and others returning from courses, but most especially, the next batch of visiting wives. That process was wonderfully successful and a tremendous morale booster.

It was well along in the tour of duty before my wife Irene was scheduled to visit. This was one of the times that I felt the CO should be near the back of the line, not the front. To ease the pain of separation, I wrote to her every day and she responded. Written words sometimes surpass other communications. You have time to choose exactly how you want to say something and if on the first try you are not satisfied, you can start again. Once the message is received, you can read it over and over.

Some have asked what in the world I had to write about with such frequency. You probably know, for by now you will have recognized the unusual dynamics that are involved in soldiering. Beyond that was the desire to continually assure my wife and family of my love for them. There was usually something in each letter for the kids; however, they always felt a little cheated when Irene would come to the "personal" part and have to say, "The rest is for mommy."

When the moment of her visit arrived and I saw her coming off that aircraft, she looked so beautiful. Our time together in Cyprus was more than a second honeymoon. We toured the Island in the Mercedes. My car radio always ensured that I was in touch with my Headquarters and I was never more than an hour or so distant. We were in the Turkish quarter of the capital one day when I was summoned to base. Irene elected to remain and look about on foot.

Irene soon found a parade. She thought, "Is this a parade marking the end of tour for the Turkish national contingent? How colourful! But what is the Inspecting Officer doing? He's kissing each of his soldiers! Well, that's a lot cheaper than handing out medals! I'll suggest the idea to Thorold. He's always looking for new and better ways of doing things!"

We left the Island for three days, spending them in Israel as guests of Canadian Ambassador McGauckie. He also filled that role with the Cypriot Government, but with it being in the Commonwealth, his title there was High Commissioner. When on Cyprus, he used my Mess as his hosting center. He was an unusual man. He looked like Mr. McGoo of cartoon fame! Those closest to him called him "McGuff". He had a great sense of humour and a kind spirit. As a hobby he took care of injured turtles. While we were in Israel, he loaned us his personal car and even gave us gasoline vouchers!

A couple of little extras on Cyprus. First, there was the problem of grave robbing: the digging up of graves to steal and sell artifacts often buried with the deceased. This was against the law and really upset the government, which was having trouble policing the Island while maintaining a war footing. The UN was asked to help. Our Unit agreed to intervene. We knew it was going on because we were constantly coming across newly-disturbed grave sites. Warnings had no effect. We had to catch them red-handed!

It was obvious that the robbers had established a warning system in the villages, so the main roads had to be avoided. We would just have to approach the various grave sites cross country. The scheme sounded like great fun, so I decided to join one of our *sorties*.

It was a good, clear night. As we reached the high ground overlooking a particularly lucrative area, we could see a man up to his shoulders in a hole. He was certainly digging fast. The dirt was flying! We were only a couple of hundred meters from him when he noticed us and recognized immediately that it was impossible to escape.

When we reached him he was still in the hole, but rather than digging it out, he was filling it in. He was literally burying himself as he did so. With a straight face he greeted us and reported that he had just come across this hole, was aware of the UN's concern about preventing such things, and as a good citizen he was filling it in to help us out! A great story!

Second, Canadians soldiers seldom go anywhere without helping in some welfare enterprise. On Cyprus we supported a small Red Cross medical/children's aid center.

At my Headquarters there was a briefing room. Once and sometimes two or three times each week, I was called upon to brief VIPs and lesser lights who were paying a visit to the Island. The presentation included the operational role of the UN forces and the current political environment in which we laboured. It didn't take long to recognize that this little enterprise had gold mine potential. I couldn't charge for the briefing, but I made sure the guests were aware of our Red Cross project and invited them to contribute to that cause on the way out. Most did and the amount raised was quite substantial.

Then, as suddenly as it began, it ended. The Battalion was back in Canada, leave was over and the Unit was once again on exercise at Camp Wainwright.

There I was caught up in a ferocious war game, but was fully aware that my time as CO was rapidly drawing to an end. The Brigade Commander umpired me out of play, so it fell to Major Kent Foster to lead the Regiment gallantly on.

I reported to Brigade Headquarters to watch the unfolding drama from the sidelines. There I tried to persuade the Brigadier to do himself in (of course, just for the war games) so I could have a go at commanding the Brigade. I argued that turn about was fair play, but he wouldn't budge. Thus, my chance at commanding about 6000 men went by the board, never again to raise its decorated head. What a way to go!

The Exercise Log read "CO 3PPCLI killed in action."

Chapter 26
IS THERE LIFE AFTER DEATH?

The Commandant of the Combat Arms School in Gagetown, New Brunswick, sent a letter to me in Victoria. He expressed his satisfaction at my posting to the School, made some vague reference to my role there, and then wrote at length about my extracurricular responsibility, the Base ski hill. I need to say that, from that moment on, he had a pretty unhappy camper on his hands. I should have stayed in Wainwright. From a military perspective, it was one big mess.

The School was essentially responsible for the advanced training of armour, artillery and infantry personnel. When the word of my move was first made known, I understood that I was heading for the Deputy Commandant's chair. Somehow that role was given to a Gunner and I got the Guns. I became the first and only Infantry Officer in the history of the Canadian Army to command what was essentially the Artillery School. It took a whole year to sort things out.

In my second year at Gagetown I commanded the Tactics Wing. Its major responsibility was the qualification of army would-be combat team Commanders. That new appointment helped make life a whole lot more bearable, but not more so than the arrival of the new Commandant and friend, Colonel Charlie Belzile. The Tactics Wing was very much a hands-on responsibility as I moved with, created scenarios for and corrected and commended the personal performance of young field Officers. They were learning to lead a combined force of infantry, armour and artillery in low level tactical settings. The soldiers involved were very competent professionals and wonderfully flexible. In a routine day they might experience the change of Commanders as many as three or four times.

Now for the good news. The ski hill made money. For the first time in the decade or so of its existence, we ended the year in the black. It wasn't that I was a gifted director. It was just the fact that with all skiers paying their way, the income was there. We Marsaws never once strapped on the boards, so I avoided building relationships which led to freeloaders before.

More good news. Baby Brendalynn arrived. The girls were so excited; mom and dad a little embarrassed. You'd think that after fifteen years of marriage, we'd know how these things happen! It had been nine years since Beverley was born and we thought that we had completed our family. Of course, there was the adventure of 1969, but that child was lost as we journeyed across America on our way to Command.

One final, sad and cautionary note must be recorded in this section. War, as well as training for war, is a very serious business. Toward the end of our time in Gagetown, three of my soldiers were killed in a training accident. They were crewmen on board a Centurion Tank which was heading for a refueling rendezvous. It overshot the turn-off into a wooded area where it was to meet the fuel tankers and ended up on a slightly downhill slope. The tank stopped all right, but when the driver attempted to get it into reverse he missed the gear and the vehicle started to roll slowly down hill. He tried a second time and failed again. The vehicle picked up momentum. Before we knew it, it had reached a small bridge.

The tank wasn't aligned with the bridge. One track was on the bridge, the other in space. The 54 ton Centurion flipped over. Its fuel escaped, hit the red-hot engine and exploded. The three-man crew was gone in an instant, as the fire sucked all the air from the interior of the vehicle. The only good news was that the flames never touched the men.

In my time in command I lost four soldiers in total. In addition to the above three, you'll recall that Rifleman George drowned in a B.C. mountain stream while on patrol. In spite of all of the pomp and ceremony of a military funeral, it's always a sad and gut-wrenching occasion.

Chapter 27
THE END OF A GREAT RUN

We were barely two years at Gagetown before we were once again on the move, this time to Mobile Command (Army Headquarters), St. Hubert, Quebec. As soon as I learned of the posting, and knowing that there would be no married quarters for me, I went house hunting.

In the end we had to buy again. This time we had a new home built, big enough for all seven of us, in St Bruno. It was only a few miles from work, but ten from Greenfield Park, the nearest Fellowship Church. Pastor Alex Shook had been with Canadian Intelligence during WW2 and had some interesting adventures. He had been taken through the lines at one time by Popski's Private Army, a real live "Rat Patrol" kind of organization. He obviously lived through it, even though he finished on the German side of the line at war's end.

As this posting unfolded, it was interesting how differently it was handled. They actually asked me if I thought I would like the challenge. I said yes. Then two weeks later, I learned that the new Commander was going to be the very person who had been at the focal point of my pre-Norwegian woes!

Needless to say I was apprehensive, but by the end things had developed really well. On our very first encounter he argued that he had to call things the way he had seen them and that is true; however, he expressed his regret over the incident and his pleasure at how well things had worked out. That was big! He went on to become Canada's first elected Senator.

My new role was that of Senior Staff Officer - Doctrine. My job included the writing, revising and editing of all military publications and manuals. Over the previous several years only a handful of documents made it to press. During my three years, thirty-seven publications were issued.

Two things contributed to this enormous advance. First was the practice of contracting out. I initiated the policy of reaching into the ranks of the retired and hiring proven professionals to draft key manuals.

Second, the ASE90 made its appearance. It was the first high-powered word processor to come into the Army's inventory. Nowadays we take computer capacity for granted, but back then this thing had people standing around in awe.

Even though this role involved only a handful of soldiers, more Officers than men, this group proved to be true to the military's reputation that where there's a uniform, there is humour. Long before recycling became the rage it is today, I had my own little campaign going. Of necessity we were moving a lot of paper in the doctrine section and I did my best to eliminate waste. When personally involved in drafting new material, I insisted on using the reverse side of old manuscripts.

One day when passing through my production room, I pulled a sheet off the copier to see what was running. Recognizing it as something which had long ago been edited out, I asked the soldier why he was running this stuff. The young man, who was brand new to the section, didn't look up from his work, didn't recognize my voice and responded, "We don't have any decent junk and the Colonel won't use anything else, so I'm running some off."

The Sergeant who ran production was a black fellow, proud of his heritage. He was always a good humoured guy. Around him, funny things happened with uplifting regularity. Once, we had a power outage in our wing of the Headquarters. Unfortunately, the hall had no windows so it was pitch black.

As I made my way along the hall, someone came toward me hollering "Whoop!" every two or three seconds. When I met up with the voice, it turned out to be the good Sergeant.

"What in the world are you up to now?" I asked.

"Well sir, it's so dark in here, I didn't want any white fellows stepping on me, so I thought I'd better send out an early warning signal!"

Meanwhile, Irene and I had long been sensing that we would go into some kind of ministry when we reached the end of the military line. Indeed, I was already studying by correspondence through Fort Wayne Bible College, in a six year program with a year's residency at Central Baptist Seminary, Toronto. Then what and where?

Towards the end of my second year in the Doctrine job, I reached my 25th year in the regular army. I was approaching the ripe old age of 45. Very shortly thereafter, I submitted my resignation dated one year thence. I was determined to leave a good taste in the mouth of my superiors. Over the years it had frustrated me to see some fellow Officers, in response to an industrial opportunity, just up and quit, almost on the spur of the moment. My commission was very much open-ended and I did not want to desert. I told my Commander that I would do anything and everything he wanted of me in the next twelve months.

You will hardly believe what happened next. At the operational briefing on the Friday of the week in which I put in my notice of retirement, I walked into the conference room and there on the screen was a list of Officers being offered special terms of service. My name was second or third from the top. When I returned to my office, the phone rang. It was the Housing Control Officer advising me that a Colonel's residence had just come available and that I was first in line. Then, in a day or two, a paper passed through my hands confirming that I was in the top ten for promotion and had been for three or four years. As I eventually saw all this, it was a challenge to either discourage me from retiring or to test me to see if I would turn my back on my call into the ministry.

Now, it was an Army policy that those resigning should be interviewed to ensure that they knew exactly what they were doing. My immediate superior spoke with me. "I have no doubt you have thought this whole thing through very carefully," he said, "But I do have one question. Don't you consider the military a big enough mission field for you?"

I explained that I felt called into full-time ministry and when that occurs, God expects you to obey. The military had been great, but it was time to follow a different Commander.

The last weeks of my military career were rushing by. Interestingly, on my final day in the service I participated in a major meeting assembled to decide on the purchase of an equipment item involving the expenditure of millions of dollars.

Suffice it to say that my military career was a fantastic training ground for my second career -- that of full-time ministry. Eager for the new and rewarding adventure, I considered this point to be "the first day of the rest of my life."

In the end, we stand amazed at the evidence of God's direction, determination to supply all of our needs and leading through an exciting, adventure-filled life. For the lad who was "born to run", it was time to "change hats" -- from Lieutenant Colonel "Boom" Marsaw to Pastor Thorold Marsaw.

What of our life in the ministry and of our growing family, which now includes grandchildren? Did the boy who was born to run have at least as much energy and success in ministry as he had in the military? Yes, that much and more, as God saw fit to use Irene and myself in His service!

Amen!

★

EDITORIAL NOTE

What happened to the "born to run" Lieutenant Colonel Thorold Marsaw?

"Boom" Marsaw took an early retirement from the Army in 1976 to enter the ministry. After Seminary, he began a home mission church in Agincourt, Ontario. Later he pastored several other churches and even assisted other Ministers while working in the Fellowship office. Thorold retired in 1999.

Did I say retired? Even now, when asked to guest minister to various congregations or provide well-experienced advice to other Pastors, it's still "no problem"! And did I mention his latest careers as author, speaker...?

But all of that, of course, is yet another story...

- Jim Pittaway, Editor

★

CURRENT MAPS OF COUNTRIES SERVED